GOVERNING THE WORLD?

Mark A. Boyer and Shareen Hertel, Series Editors

International Studies Intensives (ISI) is a book series that springs from the desire to keep students engaged in the world around them. ISI books pack a lot of information into a small space—they are meant to offer an intensive introduction to subjects often left out of the curriculum. ISI books are relatively short, visually attractive, and affordably priced.

GOVERNING THE WORLD?

ADDRESSING "PROBLEMS WITHOUT PASSPORTS"

THOMAS G. WEISS

Paradigm Publishers
Boulder • London

A new type of thinking is essential if [humankind] is to survive and move toward higher levels.

—*Albert Einstein*

Copyright © 2014 Paradigm Publishers

Published in the United States by Paradigm Publishers, 5589 Arapahoe Avenue, Boulder, CO 80303 USA.

Paradigm Publishers is the trade name of Birkenkamp & Company, LLC, Dean Birkenkamp, President and Publisher.

Library of Congress Cataloging-in-Publication Data

Weiss, Thomas George.
  Governing the world? : addressing "problems without passports" / Thomas G. Weiss.
    pages cm. — (International studies intensives book series)
  Includes bibliographical references and index.
  ISBN 978-1-61205-628-9 (pbk. : alk. paper)
  ISBN 978-1-61205-640-1 (consumer e-book)
  1. International cooperation. 2. International organization. 3. International agencies.
4. International relations. 5. United Nations. I. Title.
  JZ1318.W448 2014
  327.1—dc23

                                                                2013043921

Printed and bound in the United States of America on acid-free paper that meets the standards of the American National Standard for Permanence of Paper for Printed Library Materials.

Designed and Typeset by Straight Creek Bookmakers.

18 17 16 15 14   1 2 3 4 5

CONTENTS

ABBREVIATIONS

AU	African Union
EU	European Union
FDI	foreign direct investment
G20	Group of 20
GHGs	greenhouse gases
ICC	International Criminal Court
ICISS	International Commission on Intervention and State Sovereignty
IGO	intergovernmental organization
IMF	International Monetary Fund
IPCC	Intergovernmental Panel on Climate Change
NATO	North Atlantic Treaty Organization
NGO	nongovernmental organization
R2P	responsibility to protect
TNC	transnational corporation
WMDs	weapons of mass destruction
WTO	World Trade Organization

✳

Acknowledgments

A pleasant task arises when finishing a book, namely, thanking those who helped. I begin with Jennifer Knerr. Twenty-five years ago, she approached me about writing a textbook on *The United Nations and Changing World Politics*, which is now in its seventh edition (Boulder: Westview, 2014, co-authored with David P. Forsythe, Roger A. Coate, and Kelly-Kate Pease). Twenty-five years later, I approached her about the current volume, and she encouraged me to briefly address a "simple" question, namely, could humanity do better at "governing the world?" On both occasions, my hesitation was palpable but her enthusiasm contagious. I was especially pleased to learn that there sometimes is truth in packaging: Paradigm Publishers does not shy away from books asking big questions with answers that some might consider outlandish.

Echoing inside my head was a familiar quote: "If I had more time, I would have written a shorter letter." I could not recall the author, but a quick Google search informed me why I was not merely having another senior moment. Among those credited with coining this adage are Mark Twain, George Bernard Shaw, Voltaire, Blaise Pascal, Johann Wolfgang von Goethe, Winston Churchill, Pliny the Younger, Cato, Cicero, Bill Clinton, and Benjamin Franklin. Whoever first really uttered this bit of folk wisdom, it certainly captures a tough assignment.

This short volume is in many ways a 40,000-word essay that attempts to make sense of the many complicated and disparate issues with which I have been struggling, sometimes successfully and sometimes not, for decades. My aim was to write a provocative brief book about a question that skeptical students and colleagues alike ask with some regularity, but using as few words in as user-friendly and inexpensive format as possible. My hope was to induce general readers to grapple with the topic rather than only specialists whom I usually address with my research and writing. Suggested readings help guide interested readers toward key sources, and the citations contain additional ones for those keen to go further.

Happily, I had the time to be short. In the spring and summer of 2013, I was still on sabbatical leave from The City University of New York's Graduate Center, my academic home since 1998. I am thankful to President William Kelly and Provost Chase Robinson for warmly and generously sustaining my leave and other adventures over the years. I also had support from the One Earth Future Foundation; the Centre for Global Governance Studies at the University of Leuven; the Kulturwissenschaftliches Kolleg of the University of Konstanz; and the Centre for International Studies and Diplomacy at SOAS, University of London.

These pages reflect previous and ongoing work with two other colleagues and friends whose insights permeate these pages, namely, Australian National University's Ramesh Thakur—especially our *Global Governance and the UN: An Unfinished Journey* (Bloomington: Indiana University Press, 2010)—and the University of Manchester's Rorden Wilkinson—most recently our edited *International Organization and Global Governance* (London: Routledge, 2014). I am grateful to Polity Press for permission to draw on material from my *Global Governance: Why? What? Whither?* (Cambridge: Polity Press, 2013).

I would like to thank Martin Burke, an advanced student at The CUNY Graduate Center, for his research and insights, especially for pushing me to think more deeply about regionalism as a building block for world order. I also am grateful to Danielle Zach, who edited the manuscript. I also wish to thank friends as well as reviewers whose critical comments on various aspects of the argument invariably made me pause even when I did not incorporate their suggestions. Substantial redrafts sharpened the argument and made the text more accessible.

Finally, this book is dedicated to my grandchildren, Amara and Kieran, and to future offspring of friends on several continents. They deserve resoundingly affirmative and humane answers to whether humanity collectively is capable of governing the world, whether we are able successfully to address those thorny and transnational "problems without passports" that former UN secretary-general Kofi Annan repeatedly warns threaten us all.

As always, comments are welcome, and remaining howlers are my responsibility.

INTRODUCTION

The world is at a critical juncture. That sentence has been written or uttered numerous times and in all of the world's languages. However, it has particular resonance for what the French would label *le problématique* of our times, the disconnect between the growing and widespread perception of interconnectedness of urgent global problems—climate change, proliferation of weapons of mass destruction (WMDs), terrorism, atrocities, financial volatilities, pandemics, and the list goes on—and the rickety political structures for international problem solving and decision making. Seemingly everything is globalized—everything, that is, *except* politics. Commerce, culture, ideas, and technologies move freely; but politics remain imprisoned behind national borders. In short, while the world has changed, our basic way of managing it has not.

Since time immemorial citizens and leaders, political philosophers, and authorities of various stripes have scratched their heads while wondering, are we capable of governing the world? We have heard numerous proposals: some unattractive and offensive (e.g., empire or forced religious conversions); some ambiguous and tentative (e.g., the failed or moribund collective-security experiments of the League of Nations and the United Nations); and some premature and idealistic (e.g., an overarching world authority). While our immediate predecessors on planet Earth have customarily waffled on this essential question, we cannot. Environmental, economic, humanitarian, and political crises threaten stability, prosperity, and even the very survival of humanity.

Let us return to history for a moment to understand better why affirmative answers to whether it is possible to govern the world have disappointed: unacceptable domination or over-the-top utopianism. The "world" (often viewed as less vast than the entire globe) was typically defined by "doers" (those in power) with aspirations for top-down control over as much territory and as many peoples as possible. Numerous empires—Greek, Roman, Byzantine, Ottoman, British, fascist, Soviet, American—or the religious equivalents—in particular, the Catholic Inquisition and the Islamic Caliphate—were not especially well received by those who were under the boot or sandal of foreign or religious oppressors. With some regularity, the basis for power and control changed, and those who sought to govern the world were replaced by others with a new ideology or religion to impose. Contemporary proponents for political and religious hegemony exist, but their backward-looking and nostalgic chest-thumping rings truly hollow.

The "thinkers" (as opposed to doers) who put forward humanistic visions about how best to govern the world were an infinitesimal minority. Their messages about supranational structures customarily were greeted with laughter as well as numerous logistic and moral objections.

This author clearly is not a member of the former but of the latter camp—with an important difference. I am making the case for elements of an overarching but nonauthoritarian central authority, which is no longer premature although many will see it as truly utopian. Columbia University historian Mark Mazower's masterful overview of ideas about *Governing the World* contains no question mark in its title and argues that intergovernmental organizations are viable only when great powers allow them to be. His pessimism is palpable: "The idea of governing the world is becoming yesterday's dream."[1]

Yet it remains mine today, which is why I have placed a question mark in this book's title. My uncertainty is not about great powers but about all countries—major, middle, and minor powers alike—and the planet's seven billion citizens: collectively will we have the wisdom and political savvy to address a host of global problems that pay no heed to national boundaries? The struggle is on for the soul of governing the globe and thus about the nature of the present world order and the human societies that constitute it. There will undoubtedly be plenty of guffaws, but I urge readers to hold them until the end of this short volume.

Two decades ago, my late friend Harold Jacobson would not have chuckled. He observed that the march toward a world polity was woven into the very tapestries on the walls of the *Palais des Nations* in Geneva—now the UN's European Office but once the headquarters of the first experiment with universal intergovernmental organization, the defunct League of Nations. They "picture the process of humanity combining into ever larger and more stable units for the purpose of governance—first the family, then the tribe, then the city-state, and then the nation—a process which presumably would eventually culminate in the entire world being combined in one political unit."[2] The post-Enlightenment period was fruitful in blending science and thinking about how to link individuals in ever-larger communities. "As man advances in civilization, and small tribes are united into larger communities," said Charles Darwin, "there is only an artificial barrier to prevent his sympathies extending to the men of all nations and races."[3]

Other than a few survivors on the endangered species list—namely, the almost extinct world federalists—virtually no one believes that is where we are headed. Smugness typically characterizes perfunctory dismissals regarding the disappearance of this noble but megalomaniacal, visionary but delusional idea. The July 2008 cover of *The Economist* depicted a collapsing Tower of Babel whose apertures had various acronyms—IMF, UN, EU, and NATO—accompanied by the caption "What a way to run the world." The divinely inspired linguistic and cultural differences, which were at the root of that arrogant construction project, supposedly contained an eternal warning from on high: attempts to create global oversight and institutions are damned for eternity. That cover suggests that moving beyond sacrosanct state sovereignty is a fool's errand.

However, my subtitle suggests that *The Economist* got it wrong, that humanity is collectively able to address what former UN secretary-general Kofi Annan aptly calls "problems without passports."[4] Our capacity to manage global threats has not kept pace with their increased complexity and danger. Our task thus is to find solutions without passports—or at least ones that waive visas that impede international cooperation—so that we can overcome barriers to effective collective action. As global problem solving is not a sunset industry, it is sensible to embroider somewhat our original question: how is it possible to govern the world without a government for the world?

The current reply, by me and others, is "global governance." A short definition is collective efforts to identify, understand, and address worldwide problems. A more complete definition is the sum of the informal and formal ideas, values, rules, norms, procedures, practices, policies, and institutions that help all actors—states, intergovernmental organizations (IGOs), civil society and nongovernmental organizations (NGOs), transnational corporations (TNCs), and individuals—identify, understand, and address transboundary challenges that go beyond the problem-solving capacities of individual states. At its most basic, global governance is a set of questions that enable us to work out how the world is, was, and *could* be governed, how changes in grand and not-so-grand patterns of governance occurred, are occurring, and ought to occur.

Global governance helps us understand how a large number of international transactions take place with a surprising degree of order, stability, predictability, and occasionally—but too rarely—fairness. Every day in virtually every corner of the world, exchanges occur smoothly with neither notice nor comment. Envelopes and packages are delivered from afar with postage affixed in various currencies. Travelers arrive by road and at airports, harbors, and train stations, many crossing borders with barely a nod. Warnings about potential weather disasters are shared. Goods and services move by land, air, sea, and cyberspace. Safety and security are expected—in fact, disruptions and failures in international transactions often are less frequent and spectacular than internal transactions in Somalia, Afghanistan, the Democratic Republic of the Congo (DRC), and other countries with supposedly functioning governments. Moreover, the existence of regional collaboration—most obviously in Europe but elsewhere as well—along with the emergence of such ad hoc groups as the G20 suggest the need to understand both worldwide arrangements and less-than-global ones that dramatically influence world politics.

That largely unseen and underappreciated economic, political, technological, and other structures enable the provision of such global public goods is uncontroversial. Moreover, there are even more remarkable nonevents that go unremarked, including the fact that no children are dying from smallpox and that no nuclear weapon has been detonated in war since the two horrific explosions in Japan in 1945.

The proverbial Martians, landing in surprisingly large areas of the planet, thus would observe many smooth international transactions and would undoubtedly have no trouble in providing an affirmative answer to our central question about the extent to which we *can* govern the world because to a remarkable degree we already *do*. At the same time, the insightful extraterrestrials would be obliged to note many fitful, tactical, short-term, and local responses to a growing number of actual or looming threats that require the opposite: sustained, strategic, longer-run, and global actions.

Global governance can help us to better understand the reasons for this fundamental disconnect as well as possible ways to ameliorate the worst aspects of the current world order. Global governance offers insights into the fundamental dilemma of our current system: it provides more order, predictability, and stability than the anarchical state of international relations would lead us to imagine but also paralysis in the face of massive dangers. My appreciation for global governance resembles Dag Hammarskjöld's reported characterization of the United Nations: "not created to take mankind to heaven, but to save humanity from hell." In the ashes of World War II and in the midst of the Cold War, however, we should recall that the UN's second secretary-general was not falsely modest but actually extraordinarily ambitious. Today, so too are quantum jumps in better global governance.

Can humanity formulate a plausible and affirmative response to whether we are capable of governing the world? This book tackles head-on that unsettling question, the answer to which will determine our collective fate. "We already do" is part of my answer, but it requires another independent clause: "but we can and must do better." One of the reasons to peer through the lenses of global governance is that they offer a way of not writing off or ignoring substantial, albeit inadequate, past efforts to fill major gaps in governing the globe: in knowledge, norms, policies, institutions, and compliance.[5] Too often a discussion of global problems might well depress Voltaire's Dr. Pangloss. We clearly are not living in what that unwarranted optimist viewed as the best of all possible worlds. At the same time, we are not starting at square one, and things could be far worse; past efforts, successful or less so, provide important stepping stones toward a better future. We need to understand the intricacies of structures and interactions by numerous agents in order to learn lessons from the past and apply them to improve future global governance.

To fast-forward to my conclusion, we require a three-pronged strategy in the decades ahead: the continued evolution and expansion of the formidable amount of practical global governance that already exists; the harnessing of political and economic possibilities opened by the communications revolution that began late in the twentieth century; and the recommitment by states to a fundamental revamping and strengthening of the United Nations system.

Whether the world can be better governed also necessitates satisfying three important "catches" that accompany my resounding "yes": it can if the nature of state sovereignty expands to include more common interests; if individuals emphasize human solidarity and fairness; and if supranational authority and federal institutions, along with more robust universal IGOs, are in the medium-term architectural drawings to facilitate global problem solving.

Embracing a genuine diversity of organizational arrangements—some centralized, some decentralized—and a plurality of problem-solving strategies— some worldwide, some local—is the order of the day. One size definitely does not fit all; there are few global cookie cutters. Different institutions, partners, and rules are required to deal with different issues. "Whatever works" is thus a useful motto.

It is essential to keep in mind our starting and ending point: improvements are plausible and not merely desirable in contemporary global governance. While exploring that proposition, nonetheless it is essential to keep a sobering query in mind: can we ever get adequate, let alone genuinely good, global governance without something resembling modest world government? Responding honestly to this query, I argue, will prove to be the real challenge of our times. My response, as the reader may have guessed, is that some central authority is required.

CHAPTER ONE
GLOBAL GOVERNANCE TODAY

The first task in determining whether global governance has a future is straightforward, albeit not simple: to understand the nuts and bolts of global governance and the reasons why it has assumed such prominence among scholars and policy analysts in recent years. In 2005 Michael Barnett and Raymond Duvall characterized the idea of global governance as having "near-celebrity status": "In little more than a decade the concept has gone from the ranks of the unknown to one of the central orienting themes in the practice and study of international affairs."[1] So how did the idea of governing the world emerge?

The History of the Idea of Global Governance

Global governance might be said to spring from a family tree that sprouted with Dante's *Monarchia* at the beginning of the fourteenth century, which initiated a tradition of criticizing the existing order and replacing it with a universal government. Others who thought along this idealistic line include Hugo Grotius, the Dutch jurist whose *On the Laws of War and Peace* (1625) usually qualifies him as the father of international law; Émeric Crucé, the French monk who died in 1648 (the same year as the treaties of Westphalia) and dreamed of a world court where nations could meet and work out disputes and agree to disarm; and Immanuel Kant, whose *Perpetual Peace* (1795) envisioned a confederation of pacific, republican states. Cosmopolitanism and proposals for world government appeared also in Chinese and Indian writings.[2]

Global governance's lineage includes early twentieth-century writings about international cooperation by John Maynard Keynes and H. G. Wells, whom such realists as E. H. Carr and Hans Morgenthau took to task for being dangerously unrealistic—the "smoking gun" disproving their idealistic notions literally being World War II. The twentieth-century interest in global governance replaced its immediate predecessor, "world-order studies," which many saw as a top-down and static way of approaching international studies and insufficiently sensitive to the variety of actors, networks, and relationships that increasingly characterized contemporary international relations.[3] The end of the Cold War momentarily created the illusion of an alternative: a stable world order achieved not by consensus among different cultural and political traditions but by the triumph of a US-led or a classical liberal one. This seemed possible after the fall of the Iron Curtain, but what Charles Krauthammer called "the unipolar moment" lasted very briefly indeed.[4]

On the heels of the unipolar moment, James Rosenau and Ernst Czempiel published their theoretical volume *Governance without Government* in 1992.[5] That same year Sweden launched the policy-oriented Commission on Global Governance under the chairmanship of its former prime minister Ingmar Carlsson and Commonwealth secretary-general Sonny Ramphal. The 1995 publication of its report, *Our Global Neighbourhood*,[6] coincided with the first issue of *Global Governance: A Review of Multilateralism and International Organizations*, a cooperative publishing venture between the Academic Council on the United Nations System and the UN University. This new quarterly sought to return to the issue of global problem solving, which the leading journal in the field, *International Organization*, had abandoned for academic theorizing.[7]

For most of the twentieth century, it was mainly students of international organization and law who considered whether humanity was capable of governing the world. Those who studied this question learned to appreciate the roles of new actors and processes and to examine the dynamics of change. Lawrence Finkelstein asked, in the first volume of the journal *Global Governance,* "What is global governance?" His answer was "virtually anything."[8] The challenge in the near term is to improve upon his kitchen-sink definition and to push global governance beyond the notion of, as Rorden Wilkinson and I quipped, "add actors and processes into international organization, mix and stir."[9]

What Is It?

Governance is closely associated with governing and government—that is, with political authority, institutions, and effective control.[10] What distinguishes "governance" from "government" is that governance flows from both formal organizations *and* the informal values, rules, practices, and institutions present in every human society. It recognizes the influence of community attitudes and clubs, for instance. Governance thus refers to the entire composite system through which a society manages its common affairs, a system that may or may not involve authoritative structures.

The new thinkers about global governance realized that interdependence and cooperative institutions exist even without official bodies. Organizations such as the UN and regional bodies such as the Organization of American States or the African Union may have highly elaborate procedures and institutions, but they wield little actual power. They constitute additional resources for transnational problem solving, but they have not and cannot replace states.

Quite a distinction exists, then, between the national and international species of governance. At the *national* level, governance consists of informal networks *plus* the authoritative and coercive capacity of governments, which—whatever their shortcomings—normally and predictably exert effective authority and control in Swaziland or Switzerland, in Uganda or the United States. At the *international* level, however, we have governance *minus* government, with little collective decision making and an even smaller capacity to ensure compliance. The results of international governance may sometimes be satisfactory but not because of any top-down authority; action is, as Scott Barrett says, a matter of "organized volunteerism."[11]

In many ways, this organized volunteerism is working: existing organizations routinely help ensure postal delivery and airline safety, the provision of weather reports and Internet names. The world is being governed because of practical collective efforts to identify, understand, and address worldwide problems that go beyond the problem-solving capacities of individual countries. Private voluntary organizations and transnational business, international institutions and individuals, alliances and multisector partnerships are all part of the contemporary landscape.

But, however successful the current voluntary nature of global governance is in these arenas, we must ask if global voluntary action and the all-hands-on-deck approach will suffice for the world's bigger problems. It works for logistical matters like postal delivery and weather monitoring, but far too rarely addresses such grave problems as acid rain and ethnic cleansing. Is it possible to govern the world successfully without institutions having some supranational characteristics, such as the ability to force nations to comply?

Currently, global governance is an attempt to provide government-like services and global public goods in the absence of a world government. It embraces an enormous variety of cooperative problem-solving arrangements that may be visible but informal (e.g., practices or guidelines governing private military companies or NGO participation in intergovernmental conferences) or result from temporary units (e.g., coalitions of the willing in Iraq or ad hoc corporate study groups). Such arrangements may also be more formal, taking the shape of hard rules (e.g., treaties governing the laws of war or trade practices) as well as constituted organizations with administrative structures and well-established practices to manage collective affairs by actors at all levels—including governments, IGOs, NGOs, private sector companies, and other civil society actors. This wide variety of transnational mechanisms and arrangements means that sometimes—but not routinely—collective interests are articulated, rights and obligations established, and differences mediated.

Given the challenges that remain unaddressed by current modes of global governance, the ideas that we develop about governance are critical. Ideas matter, for good and for ill; they help explain human progress and human deprivation. As philosopher William James noted, they have "cash-value."[12] And the ideas that we cultivate will be priceless if they lead to solutions to our most vexing world problems.

Why Did It Emerge?

Although ideas about world governance circulated as far back as Dante, the current interest in it began to develop in the 1990s. Academics and policy wonks were drawn to the study of global governance at this time for three important reasons: (1) the growing importance of interdependence and technological advances; (2) the proliferation of nonstate actors; and (3) embarrassment with the simplistic assumptions about supranationalism that were then common. The first two are crucial but commonplace observations; the third is not. Each, however, helps explain contemporary views about how the world is governed.

Interdependence and Technological Advances

In the nineteenth century, the downsides of industrialization (e.g., communicable diseases and alcohol abuse, prostitution and child labor) spawned humanitarian organizations and movements.[13] Meanwhile, technological advances (e.g., in transportation, communications, and manufacturing) resulted in international public unions to address such problems as river navigation and infectious disease.[14] Both of these—humanitarian organizations and international unions—were responses to "interdependence," although this term did not come into widespread use until the 1970s. Robert Keohane and Joseph Nye defined it as "situations characterized by reciprocal effects among countries or among actors in different countries."[15] In short, it became increasingly difficult to ignore that what happens in one corner of the planet or at any level (local, national, or regional) can have repercussions in other corners and at other levels.

This awareness became even more acute after scientists began to study the limits to the Earth's carrying capacity and after the UN's 1972 Stockholm Conference on the Human Environment. Ecological threats, in particular, illustrated why we are all in the same listing boat. Kishore Mahbubani, the dean of the Lee Kuan Yew School and former UN ambassador from Singapore, used that very metaphor to compare the former world order in which states resembled separate ships in a flotilla to today's in which there are 193 (the current number of UN member states) separate cabins on one vessel.

"But this boat has a problem," he notes. "It has 193 captains and crews, each claiming exclusive responsibility for one cabin. However, it has no captain or crew to take care of the boat as a whole."[16] I would extend his metaphor: aboard our contemporary *Titanic,* we are rearranging deck chairs instead of addressing the icebergs on the horizon (climate change, pandemics, financial collapse, WMDs).

Let us look at one such iceberg. It is impossible—in spite of laudable legislation in California and Colorado and of investments in wind farms in Brazil and Belgium—to substantially slow climate change through isolated actions. We must save the boat and not individual cabins. While solving global problems begins with local and national actions ("Think globally, act locally") is an important start, it is only half of the task. "Think globally, act globally" is the requisite other half. Fragmented domestic climate initiatives are helpful but will not suffice without attaining the transnational dimensions that are required to make a difference.[17] In fact, introducing an isolated carbon tax can backfire and be exploited by an opposing political party without a global deal to curb global emissions and distribute burdens fairly among all emitters.

Widening and deepening interdependence led to softening some of sovereignty's formerly unchallenged characteristics, which had been largely intact since the 1648 Peace of Westphalia. The deal struck that year to end the Thirty Years' War resulted in the international system of political order based upon autonomous states and a prejudice against outside interference in another country's domestic affairs. This prejudice lasted into the 1970s, when new problems clarified something that previous commentaries had missed: namely, the growing inability of national authorities to exert effective control over pollution, goods, ideas, information, labor, capital, values, communications, and technology. Now, with an even greater level of globalization than in the 1970s, actions by both the powerful and powerless have effects that cross borders. As Richard Haass notes, "Borders are not the same things as barriers."[18] Even physical walls, which once offered real protection to ancient kingdoms and medieval cities, are ineffectual because no country can wall itself off from pandemics or acid rain, from terrorism or financial crises.

Younger readers undoubtedly will find it difficult to grasp the extent to which so many dimensions of the intricate interconnections in the contemporary world were not really present when their parents or grand-parents began their careers or attended university. That phenomenon is normally dubbed "globalization."[19] Some observers have argued that it has been occurring since the earliest transcontinental trade expeditions (e.g., the Silk Road) and that international trade, as a proportion of total production in the world economy, was about the same at the end of the twentieth century as in the last two decades of the gold standard (1890–1913).[20] Thus, and despite current obsessions, the process itself is not fundamentally new according to such observers, who also point out that the long nineteenth century already had many elements of what today we would call the "modern world."[21]

Other analysts, however, have suggested that the current era of globalization is unique, or certainly highly unusual, in the rapidity of its spread and the intensity of the interactions and their compression in real time.[22] The primary dimensions occur with the expansion of economic activities across state borders, producing interdependent links through the growing volume and variety of cross-border flows of finance, investment, goods, and services as well as the rapid and widespread diffusion of technology. Still other characteristics include the international movement of ideas, information, principles, organizations, and people. The result is to have "undermined the correspondence between social action and the territory enclosed by state borders."[23] At a minimum, globalization has altered dramatically the ability of states to act independently. If everything is related to everything else, then it is problematic for any actor to maintain the same capacity to act with the same authority and ease that it formerly had.

Globalization creates winners as well as losers; it entails opportunities as well as risks. Many regard globalization as both a desirable and an irreversible engine of commerce that will lead to growing prosperity and higher standards of living throughout the world. Others recoil from it as the soft underbelly of corporate imperialism that plunders and profiteers on the basis of unrestrained consumerism. An International Labour Organization (ILO) blue-ribbon panel noted that problems lie not in globalization but in the "deficiencies in its governance."[24] Deepening poverty and inequality—prosperity for some countries and people, marginalization and exclusion for others—have implications not only for justice but also for social and political stability.[25] The rapid growth of global markets has not seen a parallel development of social and economic institutions that would ensure their smooth, efficient, and fair functioning; labor rights have been less assiduously protected than capital and property rights; and the global rules on trade and finance are unfair to the extent that they produce asymmetric effects on rich and poor countries. At the regional level these institutional developments have been uneven, with labor and other social rights being strongly protected in Europe and North America but less so elsewhere.

Some national boundaries are less porous than others, but no country (even Australia and Madagascar) can any longer claim to be an island unto itself. The phenomenon of globalization is hotly debated: Was it more or less influential in the nineteenth and twentieth centuries? Does it help or hinder poverty alleviation? Wherever one stands on these divides, the intensity, speed, and volume of human interactions are new as are the sheer number and variety of actors with a transnational reach. They reflect the nature of interdependence that became received wisdom in the 1970s and has continually nudged us since toward a new consideration of global governance.

The Proliferation of Nonstate Actors: A Tattered Patchwork of Authority

The second explanation for the growing pertinence of global governance is the sheer expansion in numbers and importance of nonstate actors—civil society (not-for-profit) and market (for-profit) organizations along with transnational networks. The so-called third wave of democratization facilitated the growth of professional networks of various types that fostered communications and interactions.[26] "Transnationalism is my name for a way of understanding global governance that focuses not on international institutions or national states themselves," writes Tim Sinclair, "but on other agents and processes."[27] Not merely states but peoples and myriad transnational actors now play essential roles on the world stage.

That IGOs—the UN, the World Trade Organization (WTO), or the European Union (EU)—no longer monopolize the attention of students of international organization and law was symbolized by the Global Compact agreed upon at the UN's Millennium Summit. Although its official members are states, in 2000 the world organization had to stop pretending to be an exclusive club for governments, set aside biases against NGOs and business, and recognize the changing nature of world politics. Until that moment, as Kofi Annan writes in his memoirs, "stepping into a UN hall often felt like entering a time machine."[28]

The former secretary-general was pointing out that the most formidable remaining bastion of supposedly sacrosanct state sovereignty, the United Nations, actively had to seek partners from the private sector—both the for-profit and the not-for-profit tribes. UN bodies are struggling in an era when the national meets the transnational, when top-down hierarchies encounter decentralized networks. "Can they successfully transition," asks one younger scholar, "from *international institutions* (cooperation among states) to *global governance* (cooperation among states and non-state actors)?"[29] I wish that there were a better label than "nonstate" actors. It is preferable not to define something by what it is not—but given the prominence of states in theories of international relations, the residual category of nonstate actors is accurate and apt.

IGOs are struggling to switch from being forums for cooperation among states to facilitating cooperation among states and nonstate actors. While states pay the bills (sometimes), the world organization's prestige draws necessarily upon "we the peoples," the UN Charter's inspiring opening phrase that still represents the last best hope for billions of ordinary people. The governance stage is ever more crowded. "Multilevel governance," "multiple-multilateralisms," and "multiple stakeholders" are academic jargon, but they also capture the quality of contemporary world politics and the way that the world increasingly is governed.[30]

Knowledgeable readers may protest that international NGOs and transnational corporations have been with us for some time. Antislavery groups in Britain and the United States began at the end of the eighteenth and early nineteenth centuries. The British and the Dutch East India companies were chartered in the first years of the seventeenth century, while the Sovereign Constantinian Order and the Order of St. Basil the Great emerged as early as the fourth century. The explosion in the quantity and variety of NGOs and transnational corporations, however, makes the current situation distinct.

The *Yearbook of International Organizations* has tracked the phenomena of IGOs and international nongovernmental organizations (INGOs) over the twentieth and twenty-first centuries. The data dramatically document the changing face of the domain.[31] Over the twentieth century, more than 38,000 IGOs and INGOs were founded—a rate of more than one per day. New ones are added and old ones disappear, however, and the growth in international organizations was unevenly distributed. Of those founded from 1900 to 2000, more than 33,000 were established after 1950. Indeed, almost half of all such organizations created in the twentieth century were established in the last two decades of the century.

This proliferation was particularly noteworthy for INGOs, which by the end of the century outnumbered their IGO counterparts by a ratio of 9.5 to 1. This growth in INGOs, and particularly their increase relative to IGOs, began to pick up speed after World War II and boomed after the end of the Cold War. The data for each decade from 1900 to 2009 show that while INGOs have always outpaced IGOs, the ratio held steady at roughly four NGOs per IGO until the 1950s, when it jumped to closer to five. This number jumped again in the 1980s and remains significantly higher than during the first half of the century throughout the 1990s and 2000s.

There are a variety of explanations for this pattern. Many legal barriers to international commerce and human mobility disappeared in the second half of the twentieth century, and technical advances removed some of the physical challenges that had constrained transnational connections. The disappearance or at least lowering of legal and technological barriers empowered civil society to extend from the local to the international. The relative ease in founding NGOs rather than the arduous challenges of creating treaty-based IGOs provides yet another explanation for the more extensive growth of the former as does the existence of a plethora of regional IGOs and universal IGOs for virtually every world problem. There is a natural limit to IGOs because governments have no need to establish competitors whereas a bevy of NGOs flocks to many activities, including many with the same basic acronym and mandates but from another country or another religion. Other factors may be at play as well: "The involvement of NGOs seems to rise when governments need them and to fall when governments and international bureaucracies gain self-confidence," Steve Charnovitz notes, "suggesting a cyclical pattern."[32] Kjell Skjelsbaek hypothesizes, however, that "the relative number of NGOs has been growing precisely in those areas that are most politically relevant and in which national governments are likely to be most active."[33]

As noted, IGOs and NGOs have long been the focus for analytical efforts by the Association of International Organizations. With over a century of longitudinal data, they are the entities typically cited when international organizations are analyzed. However, this approach leaves out another type, namely, TNCs—business firms organized across national boundaries whose activities aim to make a profit. In light of their increasing import and impact, this absence is unfortunate in attempting to assemble the pieces of the contemporary global governance puzzle.

TNCs are easy enough to describe in the abstract, but a precise definition that allows compiling data about their exact numbers is more daunting. The networked structure of many modern business enterprises, which are often organized as a collection of subsidiary and superordinate bodies with complex ownership and supply ties,[34] makes it difficult or misleading to identify a single entity within such structures. Indeed, given the nature of global supply and demand along with subcontracting, it may just be that borders are not all that meaningful in examining virtually all businesses. The continuing internationalization of global investments and supply and distribution chains also complicates attempts to count accurately the numbers of TNCs; increasing economic engagement obscures distinctions between national and transnational corporations.

Even with these caveats in place, we can estimate and grasp the importance of TNCs on the global stage by making a rough comparison to international nonprofit or public-interest organizations. From 1991 to 2009, the annual *World Investment Report* tracked the numbers of parent companies and foreign subsidiaries.[35] Assembled by the UN Conference on Trade and Development (UNCTAD), the data demonstrate the relationship between TNCs and global economic activity. UNCTAD's analysts counted more TNCs during the economic expansions in the late 1990s and again in the early 2000s, but TNC numbers dropped precipitously or stagnated during economic and financial downturns since the mid-2000s. However, overall growth has been fairly steady and trending upward: on average, the global economic system added 2,677 parent TNCs and 38,579 foreign affiliates per year since the mid-1990s. While these numbers are restricted to only the last twenty years, they essentially mirror the growth of IGOs and INGOs in the *Yearbook*.

The activities most closely associated with TNCs suggest exponential growth as well. Foreign direct investment (FDI) is clearly linked to the size of their operations. As barriers to trade and capital flows have collapsed, FDI has increased dramatically, growing fourfold from the 1980s to the 1990s and another six times from 1990 to the mid-2000s. Their reach and global economic engagement have exploded in recent years, thereby pumping wealth into economies and encouraging interconnectedness among states and peoples.

It would be foolish to imply that only good things result from TNC activities—spectacular fires and building collapses in Bangladesh in 2013 more than adequately demonstrated the possible disastrous human costs of FDI and global supply chains. My aim here is not to rail against such exploitation and condemn such scandals but rather to correct the past analytical absence of the for-profit sector as an essential component of contemporary global governance, for better and for worse.

Significantly for the argument here, the immediate worldwide outrage and opprobrium following the tragedies in Bangladesh provide a window through which to observe how new technologies can be mobilized to enhance accountability, an essential component of better governance. Transnational corporations—not unlike governments or environmental organizations—are affected by the expression of public opinion via blogs, Twitter, Facebook, and the Internet. Consumer outrage put heat on major retailers in North America and Europe so that their discount clothing would not be coming from dangerous factories paying poor women laborers the lowest wages in the world, starting at $37/month. The deadliest disaster in the long tarnished history of the garment industry, the collapse of the Rana Plaza factory complex, killed more than 1,100 people but led to announced changes: major TNCs agreed to help finance fire-safety and building improvements, and the government agreed to tighten building codes and improve union access. These decentralized global public campaigns are similar to the fair trade advocacy efforts to ensure that food brought to market originates with fairly compensated labor, not slave labor. While implementation still may lag, nonetheless such global attention matters; embarrassment and poor public relations have costs for TNCs and governments. Random but oftentimes effective sounds emanate from the new social media and can serve as a kind of informal world accountability mechanism.

The primary aim of assembling these numbers is to make a straightforward if not evident point: there are more international organizations now than at any other point in history; and the burgeoning growth of INGOs and TNCs joins the steady number of IGOs whose budgets have continued to increase and whose geographical and programmatic diversification are not captured by simply counting institutions. The argument here is not the more the merrier but rather that it is necessary to grasp the past evolution and future prospects of global governance. The growth in actors permits, indeed fosters, a networked structure of global interconnections, with the various different types of partners (IGOs, NGOs, and TNCs) making identifiable but distinct actual and potential future contributions to global governance.

A skeptic, noting that international organizations have been with us for some time, may ask, "What's new?" The answer is, "more is different."[36] The quantitative growth alone of IGOs, NGOs, and TNCs over the last century constitutes a qualitative change in global governance. Setting aside questions of legitimacy and impact, the proliferation of nonstate actors clearly has meant far more complexity and many more potentially meaningful contributors to global governance—sometimes by themselves, sometimes in tandem, and sometimes in partnership with states and IGOs created by states.

The mixing of states and nonstate actors is a reality of today's international relations, but truly understanding the range of players and possibilities—as well as appreciating their limitations—and situating them in relationship to one another requires considerable mental gymnastics. State authority has been diffused in every direction: upward (e.g., to IGOs), sideways (e.g., to global financial markets and civil society), and downward (e.g., to local governments). While the familiar form of state authority is vertical and territorial, the most significant consequence of globalization and revolutions in technology is the radical and horizontal change in the sources of power and influence. While many advocates for nonstate actors are overly enthusiastic—they are complements to and not substitutes for states—today's crowded institutional terrain certainly represents a quantitatively and qualitatively different one from even the recent past.

To borrow an image from James Rosenau, global governance is a "crazy quilt" of authority that is constantly shifting; the current patchwork of institutional elements varies by sector, region, and time period.[37] Even better metaphors may be available from nonacademic sources to help us imagine contemporary governance: Gertrude Stein's characterization of Oakland, "there's no there, there," and Lewis Carroll's Cheshire cat whose grinning head is floating without a body or substance in *Alice in Wonderland*. Hopefully the preceding pages and those to follow will make the concept less opaque.

Idealism, Yawn

The third reason that helps explain the emergence of global governance—and a personal motivation for writing this book—is that professors and pundits are discomfited by supranationality—which supposedly is simplistic, idealistic, and even dangerous. Despite ups and downs and a variety of crises over its existence, Europe moves, in the classic formulation by Ernst Haas, "beyond the nation-state."[38] Yet apparently the planet is different. The European Union was once thought to be a model for what could happen in other regions and globally. Long before the EU's current woes, the idea of any similar evolution in the direction of a world federal government, or even elements of one, seemed quaint.[39]

What happened? A brief history of the period following the 1945 founding of the United Nations is revealing: The United States became obsessed with anticommunism; Europe focused on the construction of a regional economic and political community; and postcolonial countries were preoccupied by struggles closer to home and building nonalignment and Third World solidarity. After escaping European colonialism, developing states, especially in Africa and Asia, were (and still are) extremely reluctant to give up their hard-won sovereignty for a global unity that would most likely be led by the very West that subjugated them for so long.

The idea of world government has been banned from sober and sensible seminars. Universities and think tanks do not pay social scientists for paradigmatic rethinking. One of the reasons that we have lost our appetite is that so many previous visionary plans have fallen far short of expectations: The Concert of Europe's balance of power was temporary. Tsar Nicholas II's

Hague conferences to end war failed spectacularly. The Kellogg-Briand Pact to outlaw war was never a serious proposition. And Immanuel Kant's and Woodrow Wilson's collective security visions were moribund in the League of Nations and stillborn in the United Nations. Grand alternatives to the state-based order—which once were political projects with a practical interest—have been set aside one by one. Seemingly the easiest target to shoot down was "world government," which had legs in the 1930s and 1940s—with support even in the United States from Albert Einstein to Walter Lippmann, from Ronald Reagan to *Reader's Digest* and others in between—but also had few practical proposals.

After his archival labors to write a two-volume history of world federalism, Joseph Barrata observed that in the 1990s "the new expression, 'global governance,' emerged as an acceptable term in debate on international organization for the desired and practical goal of progressive efforts, in place of 'world government.'" He continued that scholars "wished to avoid using a term that would harken back to the thinking about world government in the 1940s, which was largely based on fear of atomic bombs and too often had no practical proposals for the transition short of a revolutionary act of the united peoples of the world."[40] It is fair to say that most analysts of global governance see global government as atavistic idealism that is beyond the pale.

If an academic or analyst utters "world government," it customarily is for one of two reasons. First, the author wishes to demonstrate her realism and serious scholarship by spelling out in no uncertain terms what she is *not* doing. At the outset of her insightful book, *A New World Order*, Anne-Marie Slaughter stresses that "world government is both infeasible and undesirable."[41] No reader would have mistaken her convictions without this disclaimer. However, her book's intriguing title seems ominously close to moving beyond international cooperation and toward an embryonic world government; and so the author, publisher, or both felt compelled to formally distance the book and its jacket from an entirely discredited literature. Second, the term may be invoked as a functional equivalent for Pax Americana—for instance, in Michael Mandelbaum's book on US hegemony, *The Case for Goliath: How America Acts as the World's Government in the Twenty-First Century*, or Niall Ferguson's book on America as an empire, *Colossus: The Price of America's Empire*.[42] Both discuss the many global public goods that the United States provides (or should provide) and especially its role as the world's policeman—for such authors, apparently the plausible and functional equivalent of a world government.

Occasionally international relations theorists like Alexander Wendt suggest that "a world state is inevitable"[43] and Daniel Deudney wishes one were because war has become so dangerous;[44] or an international lawyer like Richard Falk calls for an irrevocable transfer of sovereignty upward;[45] or an international economist like Dani Rodrik doubts "how far will international economic integration go?"[46] When someone like Campbell Craig notes the "resurgent idea of world government," he is pointing to the buzz about global governance and not to central authority.[47]

In short, the challenge of thinking about drastically different world orders, especially ones involving elements of authority above states, has disappeared from the job descriptions of serious analysts. And certainly younger scholars in search of credentials would not cut short careers by exploring it in a dissertation.

What Next?

Because global governance is not a sunset industry,[48] it is important to understand why the current landscape looks the way that it does. Interdependence, technological advances, and the expansion in numbers and importance of nonstate actors are certainly part of the explanation; but global governance also is on our radar screens because of embarrassment with supposedly simplistic supranationality. However, that topic cannot be far offstage but rather in the wings as we examine the three "if's" underlying my affirmative response to the query, are we capable of "governing the world"?

History weighs heavily on future options but is not deterministic. There are, to adapt Robert Frost's well-known poem, roads "less traveled by."[49] *Caveat lector*: the slope is slippery along such paths toward overcoming the lack of a central authority for the planet.

Chapter Two
Sacrosanct Sovereignty No Longer

Over the last few decades, and in spite of what you may have heard from the high priests of international relations, state sovereignty is a relic—venerated and useful to explain many events in world politics but without the magic powers to predict all developments claimed by true believers. Let us begin with a definition: a sovereign state is a political entity that has a centralized government and unquestioned authority over a defined geographic area and its permanent population as well as the capacity to enter into external relations; it is not subject to any other power or any other state. Without overarching authority (the definition of anarchy), a dog-eat-dog world results in which each state will push as far as it can to advance its own perceived self-interests.

Challenges to state sovereignty come in many forms. States may want to infringe on others in order to protect human rights and address global threats (such as climate change). There may be pressure to change borders that were set during a colonial period. Factors beyond a state's control (such as economic liberalization and communications technologies) may influence it. And ideas and institutions (including nonstate actors, regionalism, and global governance) can affect a state's autonomy. The challenges to sovereignty's formerly unquestioned primacy are noticeable not only in theorizing about world politics but also in the actual conduct and decisions by governments and their citizens. The resulting flux also means that the way the world currently is governed is anything except obvious to casual observers and even on many occasions to specialists whose ideological and theoretical beliefs prevent them from seeing new patterns and possibilities for action.

Legitimacy Challenges

The most formidable undermining of the purportedly unshakeable foundations of state sovereignty emanates from the postwar infusion of individual and political rights, which make legitimate sovereignty contingent on decent behavior. Sovereignty no longer serves as a shield that aberrant authorities can use to fend off external criticism while blatantly abusing their populations. There is no shortage of thugs, but there is ever less resonance to the antiquated Westphalian tune that domestic actors are somehow above international standards. Such a trend is most obvious in the relentless march of human rights, efforts to halt mass atrocities, and the changing character of borders.

Human Rights

Many observers would argue that the most bold and underestimated idea written into the UN Charter was human rights.[1] In a speech at the General Assembly just after the adoption of the Universal Declaration of Human Rights in December 1948, Eleanor Roosevelt predicted that "a curious grapevine" would spread the ideas in the declaration far and wide, an apt metaphor for what actually has taken place, with the results circumscribing states in a manner unimaginable prior to World War II.[2]

The experience of the League of Nations in the interwar years convinced many of the links between social and economic issues, including human rights, with peace and security. Earlier episodes outside of Europe—Germany's genocidal attacks on the Herero in southwest Africa, Belgium's onslaught against the Congo's entire population, and colonialism virtually everywhere—failed to elicit widespread revulsion. However, Nazi Germany and the Holocaust were loathsome reminders about the need for "fire walls against barbarism"[3] and served as effective catalysts for their construction.

Efforts to convert the Universal Declaration into a single covenant after World War II nonetheless set off an ideological firestorm. Political and civil rights (the "first generation" of rights emphasized by the West) became separated from economic, social, and cultural ones (the "second generation" emphasized by the East, or socialist bloc, and the global South, or developing countries). The West challenged the Rest for failures to respect political and civil rights; meanwhile, the Rest pointed to the West's failures to satisfy basic human needs of some amid the affluence of others.

Until the end of the Cold War, the issue of human rights was an ideological soccer ball, booted back and forth in an international match between East and West, used and abused in the turbulent politics of that clash. Westerners wore the jerseys of political and civil rights, Easterners those of economic and social rights. Depending on their ideological affiliations and calculations, southern players actively joined one team or the other on the field or cheered from the sidelines for whoever seemed to be in the lead. The international game was mainly a shouting match, with attacks and denunciations but little attention to practical issues. The game and playing surface changed as the Cold War thawed and groups concerned with the rights of women and children entered the stadium.

For decades, few reliable data existed about abuses in such places as China, the Soviet Union, and a large number of newly independent countries—all ruled with iron fists with little or no outside access to those abused by government authorities. Now, a host of UN and private agencies gather and disseminate information. Part of the utility of the two 1966 covenants—on civil and political rights as well as on economic, social, and cultural rights—was requiring signatories to submit periodic reports. Therefore, ratifying and bringing the covenants into force did not simply connote acceptance of internationally proclaimed standards. It also entailed a data depository at the United Nations. Since its 2006 establishment, the UN Human Rights Council and its Universal Periodic Review have dissipated some of the fog behind which criminals customarily take refuge.[4]

Lacunae in knowledge about abuses have consequences, which is why local and international NGOs and other civil society groups worldwide are essential informants and participants in global human rights governance. Moreover, now we learn what is happening in real time because social media turn anyone with a cell phone into a source of information. Texting, videos, email, YouTube, blogs, Twitter, and Facebook have the potential to increase reporting, knowledge, and accountability. For example, during the uprisings and initial aftermath of the Arab Spring in Tunisia and Egypt in 2010–2011 and again during Syria's civil war, such media spread information about and pictures of brutality that both governments and rebels or dissidents would have preferred to suppress. Those present spread messages to citizens in other parts of the country and to the international media. They also disseminated alternate perspectives on events and generated a "collective consciousness" previously unthinkable in repressive states with weak civil societies and primitive communications technologies.[5]

Stephen Hopgood's *The Endtimes of Human Rights* is much less sanguine. The language of contemporary human rights, he argues, grew out of European secular culture and American power, which are no longer as dominant as they once were owing to geopolitical shifts globally.[6] While his caution against false hope is in order, I am not convinced that the foundations of universal human rights are receding; indeed, they are still advancing although certainly have far to go before being fully realized.

Responsibility to Protect

Determining whether, when, where, and why to intervene to protect civilians caught in the crosshairs of war and violence increasingly is guided by the responsibility to protect (R2P). The idea was first formulated in the 2001 report of the International Commission on Intervention and State Sovereignty (ICISS), *The Responsibility to Protect,*[7] which reframed sovereignty as contingent rather than absolute. The authors aimed to halt mass atrocities by invoking a three-pronged responsibility—to prevent, to react, and to rebuild.[8] Unlike many other commissions, its recommendations have had an impact and have not merely been "consigned directly to bookshelves or hard drives and forever thereafter unread and unremembered."[9]

Following the ICISS report, R2P rapidly took root in the international normative landscape. The 2004 report of the UN's High-Level Panel on Threats, Challenges and Change, *A More Secure World: Our Shared Responsibility*, endorsed R2P as an "emerging norm."[10] And shortly thereafter former UN secretary-general Kofi Annan included R2P in his 2005 report *In Larger Freedom*,[11] before the 2005 World Summit endorsed it.[12] Current secretary-general Ban Ki-moon formulated his own version at the outset of his first term and publicly committed his administration to emphasizing it in his second term.[13] More than 150 heads of state and government at the World Summit explicitly supported R2P, which was included in the *Outcome Document*. And the intergovernmental agreement on the occasion of the UN's 60th anniversary was a turning point in R2P's crystallization as a new norm, although something less than "an international Magna Carta"—pardonable hyperbole in a *Foreign Policy* blog from the State Department's former director of policy planning Anne-Marie Slaughter.[14]

ICISS coined the term "responsibility to protect" in order to move beyond the pitched battles surrounding the term "humanitarian intervention." Beginning with the international response in northern Iraq in 1991, the justification of the use of force in service of "humanitarian intervention" led to circular tirades about the agency, timing, legitimacy, means, circumstances, consistency, and advisability of using military force to protect human beings. Iraq caused many to question the humanitarian justification for war, but two other events in the 1990s—the Rwandan genocide and the war in Kosovo—caused others to defend it. In both of these cases, the UN Security Council failed to authorize an appropriate military response, and the result was disastrous. In the Great Lakes region of Africa in 1994, intervention was too little and too late to halt or even slow the murder of what may have been as many as 800,000 people. In the late 1990s, the UN Security Council failed to authorize deadly force and the North Atlantic Treaty Organization (NATO) stepped in instead. But many observers saw the seventy-eight-day bombing effort as being too much and too early, but past or potential victims undoubtedly would support NATO's decision. Indeed, one of the few surveys of affected populations in several war zones reports that fully two-thirds of civilians under siege who were interviewed in twelve war-torn societies by the International Committee of the Red Cross (ICRC) want more intervention, and only 10 percent want none.[15] In any event, the UN's refusal to authorize the use of military force to protect vulnerable populations linked these two cases.

The more serious threat to international order and justice was the UN's paralysis in the face of mass atrocities unfolding in Rwanda, a paralysis repeated in such places as Darfur, Sri Lanka, the DRC, and Syria. The trag-edy of Rwanda and the dispute over intervention in Kosovo shaped ICISS's novel formulation of the intervention question. Its conceptual innovation was to posit state sovereignty as *conditional*. As such, it entails duties, not simply rights. This formulation permitted a conversation about the limits of state power even with the most ardent defenders of sovereign inviolabil-ity. After centuries of largely looking the other way, sovereignty no longer provides a license for mass murder in the eyes of legitimate members of the international community of states. Every state has a responsibility to protect its own citizens from widespread killings and other gross violations of their rights. If any state, however, is manifestly unable or unwilling to exercise that responsibility or, worse, is the perpetrator of mass atrocities, its sovereignty is compromised. In this case, the responsibility to protect civilians devolves to other states, ideally acting through the UN Security Council.

This notion of a dual responsibility—internal and external—drew upon pioneering work by Francis Deng and Roberta Cohen about "sovereignty as responsibility" in conceptualizing how to protect internally displaced persons.[16] They emphasized the need—indeed, the responsibility—for the international community of states, embodied by the UN (which was mandated since its creation to make good on Franklin Delano Roosevelt's commitment to "freedom from fear") to do everything possible to prevent mass atrocities. Deploying military force is an option after alternatives have been considered and failed or judged likely to fail.

Another turning point in adoption of the R2P norm was the UN's 2005 World Summit. In this follow-up to the UN's 2000 Millennium Summit, an unprecedented number of world leaders met to address the progress of the Millennium Development Goals. The summit endorsed R2P, specifying that military intervention to help the vulnerable should be restricted to cases of "genocide, war crimes, ethnic cleansing and crimes against humanity"—essentially mass atrocities.

By the time that the summit's 2005 consensus materialized, the message was clear: R2P was refined from a broad framework to a focus on preventing and halting mass atrocity crimes, and the consistency of the norm's inter-pretation was bolstered by restricting the number of triggers. As such, the responsibility to protect provides a range of possible responses to the most gross and systematic violations of human rights that deeply offend any sense of common humanity. R2P—like human rights more generally—seeks to cross cultural boundaries and ultimately aspires to universality. By restricting the norm to the most heinous and conscience-shocking crimes rather than the garden variety of abuses, the 2005 agreement added to the norm's clarity and advanced its universal aspirations.

Most observers agree that R2P's potential strength, like all norms, is demonstrated by its legitimate use; but its misuse also shows potential power because normative imitation is a sincere form of flattery. Abuses of the norm are often considered to include the United States and the United Kingdom in Iraq in 2003, Russia in Georgia in 2008, and France in Burma in 2008; these cases actually help to clarify what R2P is *not*.[17] R2P was not an acceptable rationalization for the war in Iraq after the original justifications (links to Al-Qaeda and weapons of mass destruction) evaporated; nor for Moscow's imperial aims in its weaker neighbor; nor for intervention after a hurricane when the local government was dragging its feet but not murdering its population.

The traction resulting from R2P's challenge to sovereignty was evident in the March 2011 use of military force approved by the UN Security Council against Libya, the first such authorization against a functioning de jure government. The NATO-led military action that began in March 2011 marked a turning point in the post–September 11 intervention slump. As the working group on R2P chaired by Madeleine Albright and Richard Williamson noted, "Libya was a textbook application of R2P principles." Their report continued, "Collective military action to enforce R2P will be rare."[18] The latter statement certainly summarized accurately what had happened until March 2011: other than modest efforts by the United Kingdom and France in West and Central Africa, respectively, there had been no serious military operations for human protection purposes since NATO's 1999 intervention in Kosovo. The Security Council's willingness to authorize "all necessary means" against Tripoli's rogue regime as it mowed down protestors may mark a new dawn for R2P.

The UN's subsequent paralysis in Syria—where everyone agreed that the death and suffering inflicted by the Bashir al-Assad regime were worse than Muammar el-Gaddhafi's, even if numbers are always contested in such circumstances[19]—indicates that the erosion of sovereign prerogatives has only begun; international condemnations are guaranteed, but action is not. In addition, the follow-up debates after the Security Council's authorization in 2011 to take action in Libya—especially the theatrical huffing and puffing about "regime change" not having been authorized by the no-fly zone—were reminiscent of earlier high-voltage and high-decibel criticism that greeted R2P's emergence a decade earlier. These debates afforded occasions to turn up the volume of lingering buyer's remorse, especially Brazil's proposal first made at the 66th session of the UN General Assembly in fall 2011 that "the international community, as it exercises its responsibility to protect, must demonstrate a high level of responsibility while protecting" (RwP).[20] Reticence and even hostility are understandable for anyone familiar with the number of sins justified by imperial powers under a "humanitarian" rubric. Former colonies are unlikely to welcome outside military intervention merely because of a qualifying adjective. Moreover, they and others are uneasy about setting aside the principle of nonintervention in domestic affairs, the basis for international society and a restraint of sorts on major powers.

Wolfgang Seibel has described RwP as "hugging R2P to death,"[21] of paying lip service while actually trying to undermine it. While tautological, or at least ambiguous and mischievous, RwP also reflected the norm's perceived pertinence and power. On the one hand, a prominent member of the global South was compelled to communicate uneasiness about the use of military force for regime change, a delicate topic for many developing countries. On the other hand, as an aspiring power on the world stage, Brazil was obliged to have a foreign policy unequivocally supportive of human rights; Brasilia thus could not be among R2P spoilers.

But that is progress. While "normatively based challenges to the sovereign rights of states are hardly new in international history,"[22] nonetheless the Security Council was largely missing in action for humanitarian matters during the Cold War—a virtual humanitarian tabula rasa existed at the outset of the 1990s. No resolution mentioned the humanitarian aspects of any conflict from 1945 until the Six-Day War of 1967, and the first reference to the International Committee of the Red Cross was not until 1978.[23] While in the 1970s and 1980s, "the Security Council gave humanitarian aspects of armed conflict limited priority ... the early nineteen-nineties can be seen as a watershed."[24]

During the first half of that decade, twice as many resolutions were passed as during the first forty-five years of UN history, a pace that has continued.

Often used loosely to mean any kind of effort to influence another state's foreign policy, "intervention" should be reserved for three categories of threatened or actual Security Council coercion against the expressed wishes of a target state or political authorities: sanctions and embargoes; international criminal prosecution; and military force. Acting without the consent of a state violates the UN Charter's most cited provision, Article 2(7), even if Stephen Krasner reminds us of the long-standing "organized hypocrisy" of routine violations by major powers over the centuries while diplomats gave lipservice to sovereignty.[25] "The strong do as they can and the weak suffer what they must" was Thucydides's comparable summary in the Melian Dialogue of dynamics in the fifth century BCE. The Security Council has approved resolutions about all types of coercion in unprecedented numbers since the end of the Cold War. The last decade of the twentieth century witnessed the increased use of sanctions,[26] and international judicial pursuit also expanded with ad hoc tribunals and the establishment of the International Criminal Court (ICC) followed by a variety of other hybrid legal mechanisms.[27] Both sanctions and international criminal justice continue today as does the most severe kind of intervention, the use of force by outside militaries.

The potential for normative backpedaling has always been present—all states, and especially former colonies, are jealous of their sovereign prerogatives and fearful of outside meddling of any sort in domestic affairs. But to date R2P's acquired normative territory has been defended. Moreover, the R2P norm has substantial potential to evolve in customary international law. Despite dissent and contestation, R2P's normative agenda has continued to advance, and doubts about the transnational resonance of the responsibility to protect have continued to diminish although not disappear. Human abattoirs are not inevitable. We are capable of uttering "no more Holocausts, Cambodias, and Rwandas"—and occasionally mean it.

Borders and Secession

Another legitimacy challenge to anachronistic notions of sovereignty resulted from softening two shibboleths that were virtually unquestioned during the Cold War: the sanctity of national boundaries and the unaccept-ability of secession. Existing borders, however arbitrary and dysfunctional, formerly were sacred. It was unthinkable that part of a state would secede, even at the request of and with the consent of citizens. The Charter of the African Union's predecessor, the Organization of African Unity (OAU), was clear: imperial borders had been arbitrarily drawn but had to be respected lest chaos ensue. *Uti possidetis, ita possideatis* (as you possess, so may you possess) was the necessary trade-off for maintaining a semblance of order in a topsy-turvy postcolonial world. Even hinting that borders, however nonsensical and disputed, were anything except fixed in perpetu-ity risked opening the floodgates to instability. This belief was evident, for instance, during the Biafran War. In 1960 the United Kingdom granted independence to a single Nigerian state of doubtful long-run viability, which was composed of the traditional homelands from three distinct peoples—the Hausa-Fulani, Yoruba, and Igbo. When the oil-rich region of Biafra sought to secede from Nigeria, only five nations recognized the break-away republic. Little external support reached the failed secessionists in 1968–1970 while a central government blockade led to the deaths of over 2 million Igbo. The separation of a part of the newly created country was simply unthinkable within international diplomatic circles. Nigeria had to remain intact.

If we fast-forward to the Cold War's end, the situation is remarkably dif-ferent. The Soviet Union dissolved into fifteen states, and Russia inherited its permanent seat on the Security Council. Shortly thereafter, Yugoslavia broke into five states, with Serbia and Montenegro forming the Federal Republic of Yugoslavia. In 2006, Montenegro declared independence from Serbia, making it the sixth state formed from what had been republics of the former Yugoslavia, and Kosovo became the seventh in 2008 (recognized by over half of UN member states but still disputed by Serbia and its allies). In 1993, Czechoslovaks agreed to a "velvet divorce" between the Czech Republic and Slovakia, and Eritrea seceded from Ethiopia. Six years later, East Timor achieved independence from Indonesia. Decades of violence culminated in the division of Sudan and the creation of South Sudan in 2011.

Territorial integrity is no longer inviolable when it clashes with legitimate self-determination. Some EU members quickly accepted Slovenia's and

Croatia's declarations of independence from the former Yugoslavia, which the European Union later endorsed. Today Slovenia and Croatia are members of the EU; Serbia, Macedonia, and Montenegro are "candidate countries"; and Bosnia-Herzegovina, Kosovo, and Albania are "potential candidates" hoping to get into the EU membership queue. In Africa, the OAU endorsed Eritrea's secession from Ethiopia in 1993 after having provided election observers for a referendum on independence, which earlier would have been taboo, just as Indonesia was obliged to accept pressure to allow independence for what it had considered an integral part of the country. Within three weeks of South Sudan's secession from Sudan in July 2011, the new state was welcomed into both the UN and the AU.

Economic and Technological Challenges

Interdependence and rapid technological advances have also altered the quality of sovereignty. Notwithstanding the evidence of world wars and the Great Depression, powerful states formerly could address effectively many problems on their own, or at least protect themselves from the worst repercussions. Efforts to eradicate malaria within a geographic area and to prevent those with the disease from entering it were qualitatively and quantitatively different from contemporary efforts in a wired and connected world to calm financial volatility or eliminate terrorism, avian flu, and acid rain. Today no state, no matter how powerful, can labor under the illusion that it single-handedly can protect its population from such threats. To rein in proliferation, to slow down runaway climate change, or to manage the global economy, there simply is no alternative to cooperation.

Rich states formerly could insulate themselves, but they can no longer erect barriers formidable enough to prevent the damage from a growing number of contemporary threats. The vast majority of politicians no longer completely shy away from recognizing that reality—except during elections. In the days preceding his inauguration, an unlikely observer of sovereignty's eroding purchase, Iran's president-elect Hassan Rohani, informed his compatriots, "Gone are the days when a wall could be built around the country. Today there are no more walls."[28]

The untrammeled economic liberalization that culminated in the global financial and economic meltdown of 2008 made clearer what previous crises like the Asian financial crisis of 1997–1998 and the Mexican one a decade earlier had not. Very much in evidence were the risks, problems, and costs within a global economy without adequate international institutions, democratic decision making, and powers to bring order and ensure compliance with collective decisions. No less towering a commentator than former US secretary of state Henry Kissinger wrote at the time, "The financial collapse exposed the mirage. It made evident the absence of global institutions to cushion the shock and to reverse the trend."[29]

To date, however, the mobilization of trillions of dollars, euros, renmindi, and pounds essentially has papered over the cracks in the world's financial architecture. Converting the G20 from a gathering of finance ministers into a forum for heads of state was one manifestation that all was not well,[30] as was the increase in reserves for the International Monetary Fund (IMF) and a change in its voting procedures to give more weight to emerging economies. While this shift is probably less than "emancipatory multipolarity,"[31] at least the majority of the world's peoples have a seat at the high table. The March 2009 G20 decision to coordinate and take robust action in response to the crisis, including by boosting IMF resources, gave recovery a chance for a year—world growth was 4 percent in 2010—but the collective effort was not maintained as austerity became the fashion. One group of outraged public intellectuals in the United Kingdom calculated the staggering economic losses from failing to replicate the coordinated 2009 global action, with "cumulative losses ... colossal—of the order of a trillion dollars in 2011."[32]

Technology has been a consistent driving force in international cooperation. In *International Organization and Industrial Change: Global Governance since 1850*, Craig Murphy argues that progress is not linear and cannot be explained solely by state actions.[33] Specific structures coalesce around powerful social forces and prevailing ideas. Regimes are typically created in the wake of crisis and upheaval and often with new technologies opening avenues for cooperation. He sees that states have established three generations of global institutions: public international unions, whose heyday ran from the age of railroads in the middle of the nineteenth century through the first age of mass production at the outset of the twentieth century; the League of

Nations and UN systems, which span from World War I to the present; and "third generation" agencies from the creation of Intelsat (the International Telecommunications Satellite Organization) in 1964 until today.

Murphy's masterful account since the nineteenth century of global governance *avant le mot* (as we saw, the term was coined in the 1990s) makes a persuasive case for technology as a driving force for change and for cooperation. Another illustration is the politics of the Internet and the impact of the mass media on, for example, humanitarian responses in Somalia and the Balkans.[34] The Arab Spring brought real-time reporting from cell phones to publicize the whereabouts of demonstrations to topple regimes in Egypt and Tunisia. The same technology was used later in Egypt to resist the winner of the first election after Cairo's revolution, Mohammed Morsi, and eventually to mobilize support for the contested military coup to remove him.

Larger countries such as the United States and China have more room than smaller ones to maneuver without consulting other states; and more closed societies such as North Korea and Iran can more easily repress their citizens than more democratic ones. Nonetheless, the point here is that no sovereign can claim that absolute control extends to the goings and comings of trade or exchange rates, to employment markets and balance of payments, to what citizens hear or think.

Challenges from Ineptitude: The Climate Collapse Case

Killing Osama bin Laden did not end terrorism; papering over the fissures from the 2008 global financial crisis did not restore the global economy; containing swine flu did not an effective global pandemic prevention system make. All of these cases demonstrate that the best that sovereign states can do is to kick the can down the road. If states cannot effectively address pressing global problems that threaten the lives and dignity of their citizens, will state legitimacy not suffer? In short, will the absence of clothes on the sovereign emperor expose naked incompetence and compel citizens to look elsewhere?

Climate change is the problem that most starkly foreshadows how individuals could look elsewhere for authority because of the demonstrated ineptitude of their go-it-alone home states. A growing awareness about the

strain on the Earth's finite resources and the resulting harm, possibly irrepa-
rable and irreversible, began with minority views from such Cassandras as
Rachel Carson in her 1962 *Silent Spring* and the Club of Rome in its 1972
Limits to Growth.[35] Climate contrarians or deniers unfortunately are not yet
extinct,[36] even if Republican former administrators of the US Environmental Protection Agency believe, "There is no longer any credible scientific
debate" about the reality of climate change.[37] Earlier projections not only
seem broadly accurate but may have even underestimated the catastrophic
compound effects—especially in the global South—of population and industrial growth, humanitarian disasters, resource depletion, poverty-induced
instability, and ecological degradation.[38] For example, in South Asia, some
climate change models developed for the Intergovernmental Panel on Climate
Change (IPCC) predict annual mean warming increases from 2° to almost
5°C (about 3.5° to 9°F) from late twentieth-century levels by 2080, leading
to an estimated 8 percent decline in rice production in Bangladesh.[39] The
projected increases for Central and South America range from 1° to 7.5°C
(about 2° to 13.5°F), potentially causing a 30 percent decline in grain yields
in Mexico.[40]

The IPCC won the 2007 Nobel Peace Prize—shared with former US
vice president Al Gore—because it advanced the frontiers of knowledge
about the climate change conundrum and human causation. What had been
a hypothesis with questionable data by 2007 had garnered overwhelming
scientific credibility and by 2014 (the scheduled next set of reports) had
become a virtual certainty. In leaked versions of various draft reports late
in 2013, the main changes were in certainty (going from 90 to 95 percent
certainty on human contributions to climate change) and tone (less hopeful
with crop production perhaps dropping 2 percent each decade). The Nobel
Committee praised the IPCC and Gore "for their efforts to build up and
disseminate greater knowledge about man-made climate change, and to lay
the foundations for the measures that are needed to counteract such change."
Following its 1987 establishment, skeptics initially vilified this global network
of world-class scientists, but the Nobel Prize vindicated the IPCC's value
and helps substantiate the importance in world politics of scientific epistemic
communities.[41]

Strategic planners normally do not ignore high-consequence disasters, even those with low probabilities—and the dangers from climate change are hardly low risk as suggested by record-breaking temperatures, precipitation or drought, and storm surges. Many view extreme weather in 2012 and 2013 as harbingers of the increasing intensity and frequency of such events. Normal citizens in those years could have hypothesized what scientists verified—the hottest temperatures in the United States since records began, the wettest weather in England, arguably the coldest winters in China and Russia, and the most powerful typhoon ever recorded in the Philippines. Nicholas Stern's work for the British government led him to see "crystal clear" evidence; he compared optimists to "flat-earthers" who deny scientific evidence about the links between smoking and cancer or HIV and AIDS.[42] Fusing climate change with security issues is no longer offbeat. In April 2007, for example, eleven retired US generals and admirals published *National Security and the Threat of Climate Change*, which highlighted the salience for national security of "extreme weather events, drought, flooding, sea level rise, retreating glaciers, habitat shifts, and the increased spread of life-threatening diseases."[43] Dramatic disruptions in security are more likely to result from climate breakdown than the doomsday scenarios favored by the media, usually revolving around a North Korean nuke or a Chinese cyberattack.

The January 2012 report by the UN secretary-general's High-Level Panel on Global Sustainability stressed the serious gaps in political will as well as domestic and international institutions to tackle climate change.[44] For instance, there is no central intergovernmental body for the environment[45] that has the degree of authority and resources enjoyed by the WTO or the IMF.[46] Despite contributions by NGOs and ad hoc coalitions, existing intergovernmental organizations within the environmental arena are fragmented; they lack leadership, flexibility, and accountability.

The human species is only beginning a long and arduous journey to build institutional structures adequate to the task of slowing climate change. The relatively recent discovery of the problem partially explains the existence of such feeble structures, but the main reason is the unwillingness of myopic governments to look at the evidence and act collectively, exacerbated of course by the need to protect corporate bottom lines.

The two "hot" world wars of the twentieth century compelled radical if temporary restructuring of domestic calculations about the nature of vital interests, experimenting with international organizations, and revisiting the principles of interstate relations.[47] The end of the Cold War led to neither institutional experiments nor new thinking but rather to an ill-informed and short-sighted collective sigh of relief. A wartime footing is required to fight climate collapse, but instead there is dawdling and no mobilization. Climate changes occur incrementally rather than dramatically; there are winners and losers; and politicians are not rewarded for long-term sacrifices. As a result, climate threats are unlikely to produce the dramatic dynamics and imperatives for change that led to the first and second generations of universal intergovernmental organizations—the League of Nations and the United Nations.

Challenges from Thinking Differently

The final erosion of sovereignty's hallowed position in diplomatic discourse and academic analysis has resulted from critical thinking. Myriad books, articles, and TV documentaries have analyzed growing global complexity, the management of globalization, and all manner of challenges confronting states.[48] As noted, mainstream approaches have shifted decidedly away from the study of intergovernmental organization and law toward global governance. This shift has not, however, erased the normative preoccupations of earlier scholars: to improve the lives and destinies of the poor; to better maintain international peace and security; to protect human rights; and to safeguard the human environment. The inability of states to guarantee these public goods was and remains a preoccupation for analysts of all political and ideological persuasions.

Is global governance merely the latest intellectual fashion, or is it a sizeable intellectual step in the right direction? My answer is the latter.[49]

To repeat, global governance is the international capacity at any moment to provide government-like services in the absence of world government—in fact, Murphy remarks that international organizations customarily are viewed as "what world government we actually have."[50] The need to refresh thinking about how to better utilize international organizations underpinned the efforts of scholars working in the 1990s on "Multilateralism and the United Nations System," a project coordinated by Robert W. Cox.[51] The stated intention was to capture, revitalize, and build upon the legitimacy connoted by the term "multilateralism" as a way of thinking about how to better organize the world. As Cox summarized:

> "Global governance" means the procedures and practices which exist at the world (or regional) level for the management of political, economic and social affairs. One hypothetical form of governance (world government or world empire) can be conceived as having a hierarchical form of coordination, whether centralized (unitary) or decentralized (federal). The other form of coordination would be non-hierarchical, and this we would call multilateral.[52]

An earlier project directed by John Ruggie aimed to substantiate how "multilateralism matters"[53] while another project challenged this traditional framing of multilateralism.[54] Yet insights from this research were unable to rehabilitate the study of global authority via a reclaimed multilateralism.

Global governance has proven more persuasive for several reasons. One is concern about the shortfalls in state capacity to rein in what Nayan Chanda called "runaway globalization"[55]—states' inability to blunt the ugly consequences of global markets and seemingly out-of-control international financial institutions. The political authority of great powers, along with the absence of authority among weak states that encounter globalization as a force of nature, explain growing grumbling by civil society. This disgruntlement has found expression in mass demonstrations during the meetings of the WTO, IMF, World Bank, EU, and various regional development banks as well as in the growth of anti- and subsequently alter-globalization movements.[56] Many have thus interpreted global governance as one possible means to manage globalization.[57]

Because of these concerns, global governance no longer gets second billing but now enjoys marquee status; it is not much of an exaggeration to claim its "near-celebrity status." And the framework of global governance certainly has made a dent in sovereignty's protective armor. As the argument here makes clear, states remain the central building blocks of transboundary problem solving and future efforts to better govern the world; but they have many actual and even more potential nonstate partners whose input and impact indicate the extent to which multisector partnerships are an essential element for improving global governance.

Conclusion

The erosion of the fiction of absolute state sovereignty is well under way. The challenges to sovereignty have come on normative grounds (especially from the importance of individual rights that occasionally trump those of sovereigns) and many other sources: the global economy; technologies; the visible incapacity of states to solve crucial problems; and alternative thinking about how to govern the world. As a result, traditional notions of state sovereignty that have remained fairly intact since 1648 are being altered with each year that passes. In the future, national interests should be balanced against global interests—or, perhaps better said, responsible sovereigns should conscientiously weigh the global and regional impacts of national decisions.

The most dramatic illustration of the challenge to absolute sovereignty is the growing acceptance of the responsibility to protect. In addition to the usual attributes of a sovereign found in international relations and law courses and in the 1934 Montevideo Convention on the Rights and Duties of States—people, authority, territory, and independence—R2P adds another: a modicum of respect for fundamental human rights. The interpretation of privileges for sovereigns has made room for modest responsibilities as well, which is part of what Steven Pinker famously labeled a "rights revolution."[58] The bar is not very high—we are after all talking about halting mass atrocities and not stopping the garden variety of human rights abuse or establishing peace on Earth. Nonetheless, we have taken a giant step in the right direction. When a state is unable or unwilling to protect the rights of its population—and especially when it abuses citizens—at least then that state's sovereignty evaporates. In the face of mass atrocities, it loses the accompanying right to nonintervention in domestic affairs.

The most familiar source of power and influence remains the territorial state. It has proved to be the political structure that human beings have found the most attractive, or the least objectionable. Individual states survive and even thrive, and the state-based international system continues although it would be an exaggeration to say that it flourishes. In particular, other sources of power and influence are growing that are not territorial but rather technological, cultural, commercial, economic, and political; they are not beholden to time zones, weather, or geography. And these other sources of power and influence are the starting point for our unfinished journey to govern the world.

CHAPTER THREE
COMMUNITY AND COMMONS

Countries and the governments that run them are part of global problems and of global solutions; but their citizens are not off the hook. The Earth's 7-plus billion inhabitants, especially in the wealthy West as well as elites elsewhere, need to nurture values of solidarity and fairness. This reality is typically ignored in discussions of alternative policies, which tend to paint responsibilities with very broad strokes—the industrialized countries must do this, and the global South must do that; or wealthy governments must do this, and poor governments must do that.

The truth is this: ordinary citizens everywhere—the denizens of Berlin and Barbados, of New York and New Delhi—also must alter their behavior. In particular, striking a bargain to avert climate collapse necessitates transformations in consumption patterns everywhere. Every car or plane trip and every flip of a light switch adds carbon dioxide to the atmosphere, and scientists believe that even current levels portend considerable alterations in climate and sea levels that will cause major disruptions and dislocations. If the planet's population had US or Canadian levels of per capita production, consumption, and waste, nine planet Earths would be necessary to sustain them. That, of course, would be a difficult engineering feat; hopefully, a new global social contract will be somewhat easier.

Here we begin by examining national and international income gaps and then climate negotiations as examples of the requirements for more consideration of the whole and less of the parts—individual, class, country, or region. The European Union illustrates elements of movements in a desirable direction, including not just better policies but also wider loyalties.

Income Gaps

The vast and unconscionable inequalities within modern societies, in the North and global South alike, led to protests in Iceland in late 2008, Spain's *indignados* movement in mid-2011, and the Occupy Wall Street movement in New York in late 2011. Like many mass movements, the protest of "the 99 percent" was short-lived. But it put inequality on the agenda during the US presidential elections and elsewhere, and it stimulated discussions more broadly just as earlier protests about globalization had helped revive the suppressed consideration of long-standing discrepancies between haves and have-nots. The 2013 "revulsion" (not "revolution") in Brazil reflected a visceral rejection of the vast discrepancies between social expenditures and the disproportionate ones for the 2014 World Cup and 2016 Olympics.

Gaping and growing income inequalities within and among states are morally as well as politically bankrupt. Burden sharing worldwide and locally means that rich populations should pay more to offset the burden of adaptations. It clearly is wrong to limit a poor farmer's basic access to electricity while many upper- and even middle-class families maintain several vehicles and multiple dwellings and waste energy and water; and dire poverty amidst plenty is not less ugly between citizens within the borders of a country than it is between countries.

Keynesian policies in the United States—first Franklin Roosevelt's New Deal in the 1930s and Lyndon Johnson's Great Society in the 1960s—and the post–World War II welfare states of Western Europe raised taxes and reduced inequalities. However, US president Ronald Reagan's and British prime minister Margaret Thatcher's dominance in the 1980s decreased progressive taxation as well as reduced business regulation and social spending relative to gross national product on both sides of the Atlantic. Such policies compounded slowing blue-collar wage growth that had already been exacerbated by outsourcing manufacturing jobs, the erosion of labor laws, and the concomitant weakening of trade unions. Financial institutions in the 1980s loosened restrictions on credit, which led to a boom in lending, including to the poor who continued consuming despite falling incomes.

Even the scathing criticism of wealth controlled by the "1 percent" is too tame. In the first full year of economic recovery (2009–2010), 93 percent of the economic gains in the United States went to that top 1 percent of earners. Between 2009 and 2011, the 1-percenters saw their incomes rise by 11 percent, even as the 99-percenters saw theirs decline slightly.

Levels of economic inequality within each country, as measured by the Gini coefficient (a higher number, between 1 and 100, indicates greater inequality), are on average highest in the developing world. Countries in the North with high levels are the United States and Israel at around 40. By comparison, the lowest levels are in Scandinavia (about 15 points lower). In 2012 the United States registered its highest levels of inequality since the Great Depression of the 1930s.[1]

The most unequal countries are in Africa—Comoros, Angola, and South Africa rank first, third, and fifth in global standings (with Ginis over or near 60). Latin America is the region with the greatest overall inequality (near 50)—including Haiti, the country with the world's second highest level, and Colombia, Honduras, Bolivia, Brazil, Nicaragua, Panama, Chile, Paraguay, and Mexico not far behind. Entrenched problems of land ownership and racial stratification have long made it the most unequal region although over the last decade expanded social welfare and access to education have improved the overall situation.

According to the *Human Development Report 2011* of the UN Development Programme (UNDP), over the preceding two decades inequality has increased in more than 75 percent of countries in the rich club—the Paris-based Organisation for Economic Co-operation and Development. However, developing countries with the highest growth rates also had the worst concentrations of wealth. China and India have been hailed as success stories, but benefits have gone disproportionately to the top. In China, for example, over 40 percent of total income went to the top 20 percent of earners in 2008. Between 1981 and 2005, the country's Gini coefficient overtook the United States' and skyrocketed to 42—and many observers believe that government statistics actually understate a situation worsening by the day. As the *Human Development Report 2013* put it, "Elites ... benefit the most from the enormous wealth generation."[2] Unlike China, the United States, and most developing countries, "almost all EU member states ... have comparatively low levels of income inequality."[3]

Individuals worldwide with various complexions are the faces behind the numbers, which are even more scandalous for those who care to look.[4] In 2010 the world's richest 1 percent (about 61 million individuals) had the same income as the poorest 56 percent (or 3.5 billion people).[5] Disproportionate wealth is held by citizens of industrialized countries, which contain only 12 percent of the world's population. The United States has less than 5 percent of the total world population but one-third of the wealth. Many economies of the global South have been growing more slowly than those in the North or China and India; indeed, growth by these two behemoths skews totals and gives the incorrect impression of overall achievement by the category of developing countries.[6] Other reasons for global inequality and the unprecedented growth in the gaps between rich and poor within and across countries[7] include such obstacles to wealth accumulation by the poor in many developing regions as weak property rights and distorted land ownership structures.

Growth in China and India and other emerging economies has lifted many individuals from dire poverty to be sure, but it has not substantially reduced global gaps in living standards. At the turn of the century after a decade of double-digit growth rates, average individual net worth in China was $2,600 and $144,000 in the United States. The major social policy headache for fast-growing, populous states is how to avoid social unrest while managing an economy that generates significant growth amid increasingly unequal incomes. The challenge in the United States is different: inequality damages the social fabric and political life. In addition, Nobel laureate in economics Joseph Stiglitz has shown that *The Price of Inequality* can be calculated as diminished growth, with the result summarized by his subtitle, *How Today's Divided Society Endangers Our Future.*[8]

Much is made of the world becoming less unequal through transfers, remittances, and investment, while the *Human Development Report 2013* trumpeted the emergence of a hitherto hidden but burgeoning middle class across the global South, including Africa.[9] At the same time, global efforts on behalf of development over the last several decades have only feebly reduced the proportion of the world's population living in extreme poverty, usually defined as less than $1.25 per day. David Hulme does the appalling math: "around 1.5 to 2.5 billion people (depending on how you define poverty) have little or no access to the most basic needs."[10]

UN Climate Conferences: Steps Forward or Backward?

Many people scratch their heads at headlines or media coverage of the seemingly endless string of UN global conferences to discuss a litany of the world's ills along with policy and institutional responses to address them.[11] This is especially true for climate change.[12] Memories of 1972 for Stockholm were dusted off in 1992 for Rio de Janeiro and subsequently for Copenhagen, Cancún, Durban, Rio, Doha, and Warsaw; and the list will go on.

Are these gatherings merely jamborees for jet-setters? Would actions at the national and local levels have happened just as often without these talk-fests?

"No" is the quick answer, or certainly "not to the same extent." These gatherings are essential to contemporary international relations. While the United States never ratified Kyoto, during the negotiating processes it committed to lowering emissions by almost 20 percent against 2005 levels before 2020 and by over 80 percent before 2050. Another nonsignatory, China, pledged to cut its emissions per unit of GDP by 40 percent before 2020. "Had Copenhagen not taken place, I doubt if you'd have seen that number,"[13] Nicholas Stern argues. While no comprehensive deal was struck, international pressure was evident against the world's two largest polluters, and they felt pressured to respond; and they have in modest ways.

The challenge over time thus seems to be to weave together a coherent governance fabric from a series of separate and partial agreements. Such an approach has precedents. David Held and colleagues argue that "trade policy provides an example of how it can work."[14] Sverker Jagers and Johannes Stripple point to another development, namely, how one particular industry has been playing an increasing role in governing climate change.[15] The insurance industry's participation through inter-firm collaboration—under the auspices of the UN Environment Programme (UNEP, created as a result of the 1972 Stockholm conference)—has influenced investment strategies and has implications for global climate governance as well. Recent hurricanes—Katrina, Irene, and Sandy—have led US insurers to refuse policies for property owners near the sea, a decision that reflects economics as well as international discussions. Washington, moreover, has helped create a pact to limit global warming through the promotion of technology with China, India, Japan, South Korea, and Australia (and their business sectors).[16] Meanwhile, the Regional Greenhouse Gas Initiative, a US state-level cap-and-trade scheme, has participation by seven (soon to be eight) states in the Northeast, with other states, Canadian provinces, and the District of Columbia as observers.[17]

Again, the multiplicity of actors and multiple layers of interactions and cooperation provide a helpful prism through which we can peer. We see reflections of global governance and how it matures or does not, how the nature of a problem and available incentives help or hinder solutions. Compliance gaps for climate change remain formidable, but we can observe small and occasionally larger steps in the right direction. We certainly cannot breathe easily (literally in Beijing and Mexico City, or figuratively anywhere), but some progress is evident in voluntary compliance with international standards as well as unilateral measures taken by individual countries.

Global conversations undoubtedly have had an impact on local actions. Multilateral processes relentlessly keep climate change on various agendas while prodding both state and nonstate governors to continue applying pressure and urging changed policies and approaches.

Nonetheless, the composite results to date can only be described as disappointing, perhaps even frightening. A widening gap exists between what many countries have agreed upon and what is necessary to reduce emissions and the concentration of greenhouse gases (GHGs). More and more experts believe it highly unlikely that the world will actually keep global temperatures from rising more than 2°C (3.6°F) from preindustrial times—the red line drawn at the Copenhagen conference, viewed in 2009 as menacing but at least attainable. A few short years later, even that target no longer appears feasible. Indeed, some scientists now calculate that a number two to three times higher is not out of the question. We will undoubtedly give new meanings to Marilyn Monroe's interpretation of "Some Like It Hot"—or cold or wet or dry—because wild variations in weather patterns are what most experts see as the most telling characteristic of climate change.

A key structural problem arises because activities that contribute most to altering substantially the world's climate—energy use, agricultural practices, and deforestation—are at the core of modern economies, and there are no immediately available and affordable substitutes for them. The world's energy consumption is forecast to increase by more than 50 percent from 2005 to 2030, with China and India accounting for almost half of that growth.[18] Attempting to alter the pricing for inputs by raising carbon taxes entails substantial costs. The benefits are hard to predict even if the fallout for politicians attempting to confront the problems usually is not. The biggest producers of GHGs, China and the United States, have not adopted comprehensive approaches—although the Obama administration imposed a drastic auto-emissions reduction program and regulations for new power plants and announced efforts to impose restrictions on older facilities. California adopted a cap-and-trade system, and China has announced a similar measure. Winston Churchill is widely quoted as saying that "Americans can always be counted on to do the right thing ... after they have exhausted all other possibilities." Perhaps we can update that to "Americans and Chinese"? In any case, other countries (e.g., South Korea and Australia) and most of Europe started earlier and have advanced further although there are signs that disgruntled populations do not wish to pay for and be ahead with measures if other countries are not acting similarly.

The ongoing "dialogue of the deaf" that began in 1992, the United Nations Framework Convention on Climate Change, is conducted with a fundamental flaw built into its operations, namely, the division between "bad guys" (perpetrators in the North) and "good guys" (victims in the global South). That binary split was enshrined in the Kyoto Protocol, which a number of countries, most crucially the United States and China, never joined. What was a useful negotiating compromise or bargaining ploy between rich and poor only two decades ago, however, now stands as a significant barrier to policy change and more vigorous action.

Negotiated in 1997 and in effect since February 2005 after Russia's unexpected ratification, Kyoto set targets for industrialized countries to cut emissions. It does not, however, enumerate targets for developing countries—including fast-growing China, India, Brazil, South Africa, Turkey, Indonesia, and other emerging economies—or call on them to limit or reduce emissions.[19] The logic, which made little sense in the first place but makes even less now, is that industrialized countries had enjoyed the time to pollute and develop; and thus they should slow their growth, if necessary, in addition to financing adaptations by poorer countries as they scrambled to catch up.

The world's current largest GHG emitter is China, and the third is India, which suggests the extent to which the current agenda should be altered. The Kyoto solution relies on the mobilization of billions of dollars in aid for poorer countries affected by climate change, which is to come from industrialized countries. Only a handful of donors, all in Europe, have made concrete pledges (of some $32.5 billion by 2012), but few have actually made good on them (about $2 billion).[20]

The global North, to be sure, is responsible for most of the carbon dioxide (CO_2) and other GHGs that have accumulated since industrialization began two and a half centuries ago. And the average person in the North vastly outconsumes his or her counterpart in the global South. For example, the carbon footprint is seven times higher for the average US citizen and consumer than for her or his Chinese counterpart. Some experts claim that maintaining even present consumption patterns worldwide requires at least 1.5 planets to survive in the medium term.[21]

Developing countries have less historical responsibility for climate change as well as less capacity for mitigation and adaptation; but in the last two decades, parts of the global South have rapidly been catching up with very high annual rates of growth, sometimes approaching or even in double digits. China as the largest producer of CO_2 has more than doubled annual production between 1997 and 2010 with predictable results: Air in the capital has been registered at forty times the CO_2 level that the World Health Organization considers safe; air pollution costs many people five years off the average figure for longevity. Half of the urban water supplies are unfit to drink. Ten percent of the farmland is toxic. Meanwhile, India has doubled its output, and Brazil has overtaken France and is closing fast on Italy. The combined CO_2 output of China and India is now greater than that of the other eight countries in the top ten and will account for half of the growth in the world's

CO_2 total over the next decade and a half; and eight out of the top nineteen producers are developing countries.[22]

This result reflects rapid industrialization in high-population developing countries—China, India, Brazil, and Indonesia—and oil production in countries such as Iran and Saudi Arabia (now in ninth and eleventh places). But it also reflects noticeable declines in GHG production in the United States and the European Union—some resulting from the economic recession, but some from new policy measures. The EU's reduction—the composite total of the twenty-eight would be about twice India's levels or half of China's—is remarkable considering its absorption of several countries from Central Europe with notoriously awful environmental standards under communist governments. EU member states collectively have made the most progress in adopting Kyoto Protocol measures—reducing GHGs by regulating emissions and establishing a cap-and-trade scheme with incentives for corporations to pollute less. Overall, seven of the nine top-producing industrialized countries decreased their production of GHGs, and the other two barely increased while the eight developing countries without restrictions under Kyoto produced over 85 percent of the world's total increase in GHGs between 1997 and 2010. Clearly industrialized countries on their own can adapt but cannot mitigate climate change, which is why concomitant actions by developing countries are essential.

Industrialized countries should in fairness shoulder responsibility for previous damage from toxic emissions—and none more so than the United States. But going forward large, fast-growing, and oil-rich developing countries will be adding most to the problem and thus must be part of the immediate solution. What is the point of an agreement that ignores them and provides incentives to continue polluting? What is the likelihood that wealthy countries will agree to finance adaptations in the best of times let alone during a recession? How can politicians in the West urge their citizens to cut back if much of the planet is adding even more to the problems than the cutbacks subtract? Countries are more likely to move if they see movement elsewhere, but someone has to begin.

While many developing countries continue to argue that they should not be obligated to adopt any binding targets, behind the scenes a more positive and perhaps even conciliatory approach may be emerging: "What appears undeniable, however, is that there appears to be a new level of interest in climate change in certain parts of the developing world, a host of new unilateral commitments, and, in some places, seemingly ambitious domestic policies and programmes for achieving them."[23] According to the authors of that statement, a host of countries (including China, Brazil, Mexico, and South Africa) have made unilateral commitments to mitigate emissions, which may do more to reduce future problems than those pledged by industrialized countries. While data are still inconclusive, actions in the global South may overturn some widely held assumptions about climate politics. New pressures from the North as well as civil society—accompanied by incentives from development assistance and the payoffs from investments in green energy—help explain the growth of these encouraging unilateral commitments by developing countries.

Cutting a deal to slow climate change will require shared sacrifices—by individuals, families, communities, firms, and countries everywhere. Immediate gratification has to make room for longer-term perspectives. While some returns on investments may occur in the medium term, the major ones will be in decades from now—when today's decision makers as well as voters and taxpayers will no longer be alive to reap the benefits from sacrifices.

The next regime for climate change may be less tidy than a universal treaty. While negotiations failed for Kyoto, international gatherings nonetheless have contributed to better voluntary compliance; and some of the bottom-up approaches have compensated for the top-down version's shortcomings.[24] For example, almost a hundred countries have registered carbon-cutting plans. Despite the glacial pace of UN talks, many of the planet's largest countries and territories—from China to California—and largest corporations—from PepsiCo to Ford Motor Company—have implemented modest emissions-cutting actions without a global accord.

The silver linings in the clouds at the 2012 Rio+20 and Doha gatherings were hundreds of side agreements that require neither government financing nor approval. "The outcome reflects big power shifts around the world," is how the *New York Times* summarized the new global governance terrain for sustainability, "and the growing capacity of grass-roots organizations and corporations to mold effective environmental action without the blessing of governments."[25] Among the decentralized actions agreed in Brazil were Microsoft's internal carbon fee on its operations as part of a plan to be carbon-neutral by 2030; the Italian multinational oil corporation Eni's reduction of natural gas flaring; the Mexican soft-drink bottler Femsa's goal of getting 85 percent of its energy needs from renewable resources; and Unilever, Coca-Cola, Walmart, and other large multinationals' agreement to eliminate deforestation from their supply chains.

The United Kingdom's prime minister in the mid-nineteenth century, Lord Palmerston, is the author of an oft-cited dictum: nations do not have permanent friends or enemies, only permanent interests. His words remain true but need to reflect the reality of contemporary world politics and more especially to make alternative calculations. Many might employ the label "altruism" to describe what is required, but that seems quite off the mark—at least if we assume that everyone has a self-interest in ensuring that progeny or grandchildren or younger friends will breathe healthy air or not become environmental refugees. The world's collision course with climate collapse requires us to recycle Lord Palmerston and pursue "enlightened permanent interests."

The term "sustainable development"—essentially growing in a manner that will leave a habitable planet for future generations—was coined by the World Commission on Environment and Development, commonly known as the Brundtland Commission after its chair, former Norwegian prime minister Gro Harlem Brundtland. The commissioners put it well in their 1987 report: "The Earth is one but the world is not."[26] That sentence certainly provides an insight for climate change—indeed, for all global challenges.

EU: Exception or Exemplar?

Europe's regional governance helped save Kyoto from failure. The EU is both a regime of regional governance and a regional actor within the system of global governance. It agrees upon European norms and policies and propagates them globally, and it transplants global ones into Europe. Among developed economies, the EU's members have taken the lead in pushing ahead on climate negotiations, and the continent's registered progress enhances its credibility when the EU lobbies others to engage more actively in taking measures to make even a modest dent in the problem.

The European Commission has introduced many climate-related initiatives since 1991, when it issued the first European Economic Community (EEC) strategy to limit CO_2 emissions and improve energy efficiency. Policies have included a directive to promote electricity from renewable energy, voluntary commitments by car makers to reduce CO_2 emissions by 25 percent, and proposals on the taxation of energy products. The European Union has long been committed to international efforts to tackle climate change; and it has felt and expressed the obligation to set an example through robust policy making at home. A comprehensive package of policy measures to reduce greenhouse gas emissions was initiated through the European Climate Change Programme (ECCP). Each EU member state has also put in place its own domestic actions that build on the ECCP measures or complement them. The 2005 European Emissions Trading Scheme has reduced GHGs; and other EU policies being put in place include carbon capture and national targets for introduction of renewable energy sources.[27]

Notwithstanding struggles over political unity and the tattered euro—which reflect long-standing tensions between supranationalism and intergovernmentalism that are especially difficult to ignore during hard economic times—the European Union is the largest and most integrated supranational experiment to date. This region is, by a long shot, not only the most integrated but also the location where regionwide institutions and rules play the most important part in the daily lives of citizens, where budgets and regulations rather than war and strife are the biggest problems. As such, it provides lessons for addressing climate change and other problems as well.

In particular, an underappreciated dynamic of the European experiment is its impact on loyalties long before the 2009 Treaty of Lisbon created the European Union and abolished the European Community (EC). The 1951 Treaty of Paris began slowly with economic integration for coal and steel (in the ECSC, the European Coal and Steel Community) but over time added social and minimal security features under a revamped and enlarged European Economic Community (established in 1957 by the Treaty of Rome and sometimes shortened to European Community, even before it was so officially christened in 1993). While no model is universal—and the ongoing crisis suggests the difficulty of maintaining common sympathies without the added strains of extending them to the planet—the European experience with "identity" still resonates and provides insights into improving global governance. Beyond the rhetorical emphasis on a common fate, value changes spur supranational integration by constraining perceptions about whether other member states are threatening.

If grouped as a "country" for purposes of climate change data, Europe is the planet's third-largest economy (after the United States and China) and the third-largest polluter (after China and the United States). The headlines about Europe's recent troubles are less salient than the continent's long-standing history of cooperation. It is worth revisiting here Ernst Haas's definition of "integration," which is a process "whereby political actors in several, distinct national settings are persuaded to shift their loyalties, expectations and political activities toward a new center."[28]

Most observers emphasize the political processes of gradually constructing new institutions, but the social processes of slowly altering individual and national loyalties are also salient—what we might call the "socialization" of European integration. Skeptics undoubtedly will roll their eyes. However, they might pause and reflect on social processes that can engender increased collective identity among states and their citizens, with clear consequences for effective international public policy and institution building. The European experience provides ample evidence of an increasing structural similarity among states arising from the acceptance of membership norms; the perception of common fate stemming from transnational problems such as climate change, necessitating collaboration and coordination at the regional or global levels; and the continuing spread of common values among members of civil society and transnational networks of epistemic communities.

Since World War II, we have witnessed increasing similarity among states, especially within the North Atlantic and even more especially within the European Union but elsewhere as well.[29] The internalization of democratic values and human rights norms generates not only acceptable forms of representation and accountability but also domestic behavioral constraints. Collective identification leads states to perceive others as more like themselves and part of a self-identifying group. Western democracies have expanded Benedict Anderson's "imagined communities"[30] beyond the confines of the state. Increasing similarity—particularly in human rights and in the values, institutions, and processes of democratic governance—has resulted in a zone of peace and cooperation in the North Atlantic, and more especially within the EU's contiguous states. The 2012 Nobel Peace Prize specifically singled out over six decades of the European Union's contributions "to the advancement of peace and reconciliation, democracy and human rights."

The domestic institutional transparency necessary for effective democracy generates increased expectations that leaders signal their intentions, and domestic debates often oblige them to clarify goals. Democratic peace theorists show that less violent external behavior results when this transparency occurs. A competing academic group, the constructivists, believes that peace results not from institutional transparency per se but from the collective identity that those institutions represent, particularly in the North Atlantic since 1945 and even more particularly in Europe since 1989. Whatever one's academic inclinations, the understandings of democracy and human rights, and the shared identity that they encourage, have generated a security community in Europe with significant trust among members, a high degree of institutionalization, and a tempering of formal anarchy. That is, elements of what international relations theorist Emanuel Adler dubbed a "post-sovereign system"[31] already exist within the EU—and the argument could be extended to the West, though the focus here is on Europe as an illustration of regional building blocks for global governance.

Could a similar dynamic[32] kick in on a wider scale because of shared concerns about climate change? Climate change may wreak havoc on the world's ecosystems and socioeconomic fabric, catalyzing a vicious downward spiral of "global bads" especially in the poorest parts of the world.[33] Natural and humanitarian disasters could mean widespread political instability. Poverty and marginal existence in many African, Asian, Latin American, and Middle Eastern countries could worsen and lead to collapsing states. Conflicts could arise from already fragile areas with declines in food production, increases in communicable diseases, and burgeoning numbers of displaced persons. The International Organization for Migration, for example, estimates that environmental deterioration alone could generate a staggering 200 million migrants by 2050,[34] an estimate based on increases in temperatures that already seem woefully underestimated. It takes very little imagination to foresee increased war, extremism, and authoritarianism.

States can be drawn into cooperation to solve these threats in two ways: an appeal to common interests (goals that all players desire) or an appeal to common aversions (outcomes that all players want to avoid). But each type of appeal involves a different conundrum. The dilemma of common interests occurs when the most rational course of action for individual actors leads to outcomes that are mutually undesirable. Solving this dilemma requires *collaboration* among the players, including forums for negotiations and compromises and especially monitoring mechanisms and perhaps enforcement procedures. Otherwise, states will fear cheating and shy away from participation in the common enterprise.

The appeal to common aversions involves a different type of dilemma, which arises when states share a desire to avoid an outcome with recognized negative consequences but players have no automatic most preferred outcome.[35] This instance requires *coordination*, which is less difficult than collaboration because there are no problems with policing or compliance; once a solution is agreed, no state can improve its position by cheating. Actors bear the costs of their own nonparticipation (sometimes by voting with their feet) and consequently tend to monitor themselves. The primary obstacle is agreeing on a common solution in the first place instead of the constant concern to ensure compliance subsequently, which is inherent to dilemmas of common interest.[36]

The gradual intensification of collaboration and expansion of membership from the six-country European Coal and Steel Community in 1951 to today's twenty-eight-member European Union is an example of solving a dilemma of common interests—postwar economic recovery and German rehabilitation. The creation and steadfastness since 1949 of NATO is an illustration of common aversion (cohesion against the Soviet Union). In both cases collaboration and coordination stimulated increased collective identity, which enabled both the EU and NATO to outlast the dilemmas that provoked their creation and pursue new collective purposes as well as add members that sought to be part of the common enterprise. Benefits far outweighed costs measured in terms of financial contributions or loss of autonomy. Collaboration and certainly coordination proved to be bargains.

Moving toward common-interest calculations and collaboration based on positive benefits for the planet will strike critics and cynics as Pollyannaish; but coping with the consequences of severe weather changes, resource wars, and mass migrations could mobilize at least coordination to avert disruptive and dangerous common threats. The Earth's warming will not be uniform among countries and socioeconomic groups; the global South will suffer the brunt of the consequences. However, our common interests and aversions could be strong enough to find solutions to dilemmas, and these solutions will have to be, essentially, systems of global governance. Institutions and protocols are necessary to prevent actors from cheating or reneging on global agreements in order to reap short-term economic benefits.[37] The defining feature to date of global environmental governance—the strengths and achievements as well as the weaknesses and failures—has been the development of multilateral environmental agreements under UN auspices. To counter climate change effectively, far more robust monitoring and enforcement will be required.

If dilemmas are threatening enough, a critical number of states and nonstate actors may come to perceive their common fates as being more significant than their differences. If individual welfare (in the form of avoiding a catastrophe) is dependent upon the group's common approaches, collective and individual interests and aversions may coincide. Such developments might affect not only behavior—in the shape of creating alliances against calamities—but also identities.

However, cooperation will not automatically translate into the type of identity change that we have seen in Europe and the North Atlantic until threats are acute and long-lasting enough to jar key actors out of traditional postures and beyond inertia. We should recall, for instance, that the perceived common fate among allied states in the immediate aftermath of World War I was only temporary; it was insufficient to lead to the kind of profound identity and behavioral changes that followed World War II, grew steadily, and accelerated after the Cold War.

Therefore, until the security consequences of climate change become even more severe—for instance, more floods in Australia and Sandy-like disasters in the United States as well as more typhoons and tsunamis in Asia and Darfur-like wars in Africa—only the most superficial modifications in interstate cooperation will result. However, if security and humanitarian threats become grave, frequent, and persistent enough, they could stimulate the sort of collective identification and even collaboration on a regional or eventually global scale that has so far been confined to the EU and North Atlantic. That is, things may very well have to get worse before they get better.

Conclusion

In order to solve the growing global crises, we need not just government treaties but a change in individuals: a sense of solidarity and fairness resulting from disgust with income inequalities and from the need to deal with climate collapse. Changes in personal consumption and lifestyle are not unrelated to requisite societal changes. Here too hints of progress are present. Desirable changes in individual, family, and community decisions are happening, albeit too slowly.

Readers will bear with this political scientist for a moment as I make the case that the gradual movement from an international society of "rivals" toward a world society of "friends" seems plausible, beginning with a more cosmopolitan and compelling approach to protect the planet's ecosystems under European leadership. Such an evolution would mean a different and more mature anarchy from the one in international relations textbooks. In that quintessentially Hobbesian culture, individual states perceive others as "enemies," actively seek the destruction of competitors, and respond to threats violently. In the Lockean culture of today's international system, however, relationships are not so much among enemies as among "rivals." Among rivals, mutual recognition is provided, the right of each to survive is acknowledged, the potential for cooperation is present, and a system of rules is in place. But there is still competition, and war remains a policy option.

A Kantian culture, however, would characterize relations among "friends." Among friends, interactions among states involve occasional but nonviolent conflict, and sustained cooperation is the rule rather than the exception. That is where we must head, and in 2012 the Nobel Committee acknowledged the existence of such amity in Europe.

The current aberrant distribution of world wealth and disproportionate consumption of resources are not simply ethically but also politically and environmentally unsustainable. It is plausible for the rich to believe that they can be unaffected by global inequalities and thus ignore them. Yet such wrong-headed myopia is not an option where climate breakdown is concerned. Changing a light bulb, riding a bike, and recycling are first steps. The next is imagining ourselves as stewards in a global democracy and acting as proxies across space, time, and class; we represent not only the poor and those living in low-lying areas but also their great-grandchildren as well as ourselves.

Europe can accelerate the pace, and other regions can catch up as part of a recipe for governing the world. The logical dynamic would be to embrace that world as a shared point of departure—after the family, country, and regional neighborhoods—and to establish organizational structures that are better suited and more able to meet the challenges of an increasingly crowded planet.

CHAPTER FOUR
INTERGOVERNMENTAL ORGANIZATIONS THAT WORK

Despite the need for them that is so apparent in these pages, current inter-governmental organizations are flimsy; they are without human and financial resources commensurate with the size of the transborder problems that they are supposed to address. Even such powerful ones as the UN Security Council and the World Bank often lack funds or authority or both. Other organizations are under construction or are not up to current building codes (so to speak); still others have architectural plans on drawing boards with only a prototype, not the real thing, to address gargantuan demands. As indicated earlier, it is not so much the numbers of IGOs that is the concern but rather feeble mandates, inadequate resources, and no autonomy. We require better, not more, IGOs.

Global governance is uneven, giving the impression of coverage but often with too little practical effect. Appearances can be not only deceiving but also deadly; a well-populated institutional terrain can mask a lack of coherence, substance, and accomplishment. We may feel virtuous and persuade ourselves that we are making progress when actually we are treading water, wasting time and energy rather than moving swiftly toward safety; we may even be drowning what we are trying to rescue.

The past quarter century has witnessed a sea-change in knowledge, norms, and policies to address some of the planet's ills. We are not starting from scratch. Yet steps in the right direction must find a home within effective institutional structures if responses are to avoid being ad hoc, episodic, idiosyncratic, and ultimately inadequate. Collective efforts backed with financial resources and qualified people have clout, whereas those without do not.

There exists a theoretical distinction between "organization" and "institution." Oran Young tells us that "organizations" are material entities, "possessing physical locations (or seats), offices, personnel, equipment, and budgets."[1] For many specialists, the word "institutions" is not a synonym for "organizations." Konrad von Moltke views "institutions" as "social conventions or 'rules of the game,' in the sense that marriage is an institution, or property, markets, research, transparency or participation."[2] However, a more commonsense use of both terms is structures reinforced by rules and norms, which is why most nonspecialist audiences and virtually all media accounts employ the two terms interchangeably.

The emphasis here is on the weaknesses or absence of formal structures, backed by public international law and norms, for coordinating state decision making and action. In short, we need global IGOs, especially ones with universal membership, that work. Before building the next generation of such structures, however, three widespread construction myths should be demolished.

Myth 1: Only States Wield Power

As we know, the starting point for virtually all analyses of world politics is the centrality of sovereignty and the role of states that exercise their hard (coercive) and soft (attractive) power. IGOs have tasks delegated to them by states, whose whims often determine their focus. Such organizations are functionally reduced to their technical accomplishments and their staff to puppets. Every first-term student of international relations is taught that states are powerful, IGOs are not; states are principals, IGOs are agents. Meanwhile

TNCs and NGOs are subject to the authority of the states in which they are incorporated and operate.

We know who is in charge, or do we?

Power is not confined to states. This fact is the most neglected topic in global governance. Customarily we are too tethered to Robert Dahl's classic 1961 definition in *Who Governs?*—the direct control by one actor over another so that one actor compels another to do something that it does not want to do.[3] As such, conversations typically concentrate on guns or money, on breaking kneecaps or at least twisting arms.

But power in world politics works in ways that cannot be captured by a simple formula of material resources controlled by states. Over time, values and norms are internalized. Compliance may start with coercion but may shift toward self-interest in the longer term. An essential objective in analyzing contemporary global governance is to identify the conditions under which power is and could be exercised.

While "practically all usages of governance lack a discussion of power,"[4] it does not, despite Mao Zedong's 1938 counsel to Chinese revolutionaries, only grow out of the barrel of a gun. The 2005 essays in *Power in Global Governance* edited by Michael Barnett and Raymond Duvall advanced thinking because of their in-depth parsing of how different types of power function. The contributors used a broad and sensible approach that includes "a consideration of the normative structures and discourses that generate different capacities for actors to define and pursue their interests and ideals."[5] In particular, they examined four types of power: compulsory (the exercise of direct control of one actor over another); institutional (more diffuse, the exercise of indirect control over other actors that are socially distant); structural (the constitution of capacities and interests of actors in relation to one another, or where they are in the international system); and productive (the creation of meaning and significance through diffuse social relations and discursive practices).

In the contemporary world, state power is dispersed vertically across various levels of government in different territorial locations and horizontally to nonstate actors. They may exercise power in subtle or unsubtle ways that typically are obscured or even missed altogether when peering at international relations through state-centric lenses—which, in fact, are closer to blinders than magnifying glasses.

Yet nonstate actors sometimes are in a position to exercise even compulsory power over states. For instance, TNC investments can overcome objections by states and shape global economic policies. The International Committee of the Red Cross can influence the survival prospects of forcibly displaced persons and the policies of the states that harbor them. In such weak states as Afghanistan, Haiti, and South Sudan, humanitarian and development organizations can command considerable power by their material resources alone. "They can often be seen as forging a separate and exclusive non-state or 'petty' sovereignty that operates to a large extent separately from and sometimes in opposition to the state and other national organisations and power-holders."[6] Moreover, IGOs with financial muscle—especially the World Bank, IMF, and WTO—have the leverage to shape the policies and prospects of many client states, industrialized and developing alike.

In addition to material resources, power also comprises symbolic and normative influence when IGOs and NGOs employ their expertise, moral stature, and legal authority to induce or even compel states and others to alter their behavior. For instance, judgments from Moody's Investors Service and Standard & Poor's Ratings Group are authoritative enough to cause market responses.[7] Private regulatory initiatives govern supply chains across the globe to set environmental, food safety, and social standards to such an extent that private rather than public standards are the prime determinants of access to many Western markets.[8] And even for security issues such as piracy, a hybrid private-public initiative like the Contact Group on Piracy off the Coast of Somalia (CGPCS) has been effective in mitigating that particular crime, which governments or shipping and insurance companies could not achieve their own.[9]

In reality, the ability to secure deference (a subtler way to think about power) is obvious from these and other examples. How can we explain that IGOs, NGOs, and TNCs exercise control over actors including states? How have we largely failed to appreciate that the sum of their relationships truly helps shape important outcomes? Analysts often discuss global governance as a process but too rarely the processors. Thomas Risse reminds us why such ignorance is a handicap: "It is a truism that social reality does not fall from heaven, but that human agents construct and reproduce it through their daily practices."[10]

A 2010 volume edited by Deborah Avant, Martha Finnemore, and Susan Sell is pertinently titled *Who Governs the Globe?* The contributors focus on "global governors" who, indeed, have not fallen from heaven but are "authorities who exercise power across borders for purposes of affecting policy."[11] Human agents exercise power across borders by flagging issues, setting agendas, establishing rules, evaluating outcomes, publicizing and monitoring results, and proposing adjustments. Their ammunition is impressive albeit different from the firepower and range of military weapons, which are easier to quantify and usually preoccupy those who measure such things.

Related to the power of institutions and their ideas is David Singh Grewal's concept of "network power." In a globalizing world, standards emerge and gain prominence, thereby making alternatives less attractive. A network is a group of people connected in such a way as to make cooperation possible; a standard defines the way that they are linked in a network (i.e., the shared norm or practice that permits mutual access and facilitates cooperation). In this way network power reflects the ability of a successful standard to foster cooperation among members. This type of power is an underappreciated dynamic in global governance. Leverage results from filling normative and policy gaps that entangle states and nonstate actors alike, not necessarily through collective decision making by sovereigns but rather "the accumulation of decentralized, individual decisions that, taken together, nonetheless conduce to a circumstance that affects the entire group."[12]

In the 1995 inaugural issue of the journal *Global Governance,* James Rosenau explored "command-and-control" mechanisms.[13] Too few analysts since have examined such tools in the arsenal of global governance. Command-and-control's origins in military science typically imply top-down authority. But supplementing the realities of interdependence and the impact of proliferating actors with subtler notions of power and authority opens up the possibility for actors other than states to exercise in both subtle and not-so-subtle ways.

Our central global governance puzzle already is less puzzling. A surprising number of elements of predictability, stability, and order are present in the contemporary international system despite the absence of central authority. The contributions and leverage of many IGOs, NGOs, and TNCs are hiding in plain sight.

Myth 2: Global Incentives Do Not Work

In a national context, the kinds of threats confronting the planet typically would be addressed by a government. If not, it would be booted out—through elections or a coup d'état. But there are no global authorities to replace; we need to find other ways to proceed.

Economists emphasize incentives to stimulate the provision of goods and services that the market does not; and improved global governance is held back without incentives for global public goods whose benefits are "non-excludable" and "non-rival." These technical terms mean that the use of a particular good or service by one user does not limit its enjoyment by others. Whether a country and its citizens contribute to the creation or use of global public goods, there are no additional costs for other beneficiaries.

Improving global governance confronts the classic free-rider problem—namely, that those who do not pay can still benefit reduces the incentives to create and sustain public goods.[14] Why pay if someone else will? Why pay if no one else will? A central question is how to allocate the burden of raising revenue to finance global public goods, which are underprovided when they are provided at all.

Incentives are not tangential but central to global governance, another underappreciated and under-researched dynamic. Scott Barrett addressed these issues in *Why Cooperate?* He goes beyond net gains from international cooperation and probes the range of possible reactions from states when the costs and benefits of cooperation are distributed in various ways. Barrett chaired the International Task Force on Global Public Goods, which concluded, "It shows that some global public goods can only be supplied if every country cooperates; that many need the cooperation of only certain key countries; that most, but not all, require financing; that some can be supplied by mutual restraint or coordination; and that others demand only a single best effort."[15] Although few examples replicate the commission's three ideal types, they help clarify why one-size-fits-most definitely does not fit all, why different strategies are required to address different problems.

Barrett gives examples of each of these situations. He begins with the single-best-effort scenario: the hypothetical case of an asteroid hurtling toward Earth. As survival is at stake, free-riding is irrelevant for the most capable countries; they act and pay the bill. Negotiations are unnecessary because a single active and targeted intervention, not extended cooperation, is necessary and sufficient to counter the impending threat. Helpful in clarifying the argument, there are no real-world examples of what amount to a single-best effort although the National Aeronautics and Space Administration (NASA) has announced a competition for ideas about what could be a single-best effort someday, "NASA Asteroid Grand Challenge."

A second scenario is one that requires active participation by every country but emphasizes the weakest links. Here, we have a dramatic real-world success: the eradication of smallpox in 1977, which many calculate as the best global collective investment ever. Every country had an incentive to cooperate once all other countries went along, especially by the time that the only three with registered cases (India, Bangladesh, and Ethiopia) were assisted by international "flying squads." The modest investment of what amounted to about $300 million at the time (one-third from international sources and two-thirds from afflicted countries, and at the time the price tag for three fighter jets) saves billions annually by avoiding the need to purchase vaccine, support its administration, and apply international regulations. In this instance, incentives worked.

The third and most problematic scenario is one in which coordinated, aggregate efforts from virtually every state are required. Unfortunately, this scenario most closely resembles most of today's pressing global threats, complicated by the fact that the costs and benefits of addressing the issue are extremely varied, depending on the country and region. Climate change may take centuries (or at least decades) to unfold; countries will be affected in numerous ways (indeed, some will benefit); investments for other important issues must be reduced or reallocated; and contributions by individuals are laudable but do not produce results. Some incentives are inadequate, others counterproductive. For instance, acid rain moves across borders, and my switching to an electric vehicle or bicycle to commute may not improve noticeably the environment nearby and far less the planet's overall statistics.

In fact, the political opposition may even exploit initiatives to impose a carbon tax—which is why only a suicidal US politician dares propose a tax on gasoline, the clearest way to reduce emissions when the cost of petrol is half what any European pays at the pump.

Barrett's work thus provides additional reasons to emphasize global intergovernmental organizations that work: "Free riding thus appears to be a more complicated and challenging phenomenon than it is commonly taken to be.... Global public goods are not all alike, and the differences that distinguish one type from another create contrasting *incentives* for provision."[16] One-size-fits-all prescriptions rarely yield satisfactory results. Altruism may be helpful to alleviate the worst aspects of poverty irrespective of what welfare recipients or poor people themselves contribute. But incentives, not altruism, are necessary to entice adequate responses for most global threats. Thinking through global public goods and free-riding provides additional reasons to construct mechanisms that create incentives for states to take action to address global problems.

The overarching reasons to establish institutions that work come from the nature of the world that we are attempting to and can govern. "The relentless imperatives of rising global interdependence," as Daniel Deudney and John Ikenberry argue, "create powerful and growing incentives for states to engage in international cooperation."[17] Let's hope so.

It is important to emphasize that it is not cooperation per se but *appropriate* types of cooperation that require incentives. We usually equate global governance with activities that are hard to dislike—in particular, cooperation across borders or partnerships among conflicting parties. But Adolf Hitler's Third Reich collaborated with Josef Stalin's Soviet Union in 1939 to invade Poland; belligerents from rival ethnic groups in the Democratic Republic of the Congo sometimes cooperate to rape and plunder; and the National Rifle Association reaches out to many partners to keep guns smoking in the United States. Clearly there are incentives for the "dark side" of cooperation.

Myth 3: Supranational Organizations Are a Pipe Dream

A long lineage of realists laments, in John Mearsheimer's oft-cited words, "the false promise of international institutions."[18] International organizations and law are epiphenomena and superficial, so the argument goes, and order comes only from the state power behind them. One of the most implausible false promises, according to virtually all such critics, is movement toward overarching authority. Those who dismiss supranationalism do so for one of two reasons: infeasibility or undesirability.

Many who attack the notion are not necessarily antagonistic but rather find the idea far-fetched. It is worthwhile citing two intellectual titans whose books are classics on international relations reading lists. Hans Morgenthau was categorical in *Politics among Nations*: "There is no shirking the conclusion that international peace cannot be permanent without a world state, and that a world state cannot be established in the present moral, social, and political conditions of the world."[19] Kenneth Waltz was just as clear in his *Man, the State, and War*: "World government is the remedy for world war. The remedy, though ... unassailable in logic, is unattainable in practice."[20]

However, impracticality pales beside broadsides from ideologues who castigate proponents of central authority as babes in the woods. The unmanageable mammoth of world government risks destroying individuality and creativity. An emperor of yore would have been jealous of such global reach and overwhelming power, according to this logic. In the vivid imaginations of the most mindless of critics, UN-controlled drones and black helicopters would crush dissenters.

Considering that democracy and accountability require manageable dimensions, a less fantasy-ridden view comes from those who see limits to the scale of political communities; and for them a modicum of homogeneity is necessary to make one work. From this perspective, world government definitely is an outlier. Michael Walzer, for instance, objects that a unified world state would leave too little room for meaningful political, social, and cultural interactions.[21]

A striking feature of the contemporary world—directly relevant for determining the extent to which we can govern the world—is the existence of denser institutional, policy, and normative frameworks within regional society as opposed to international society. The European Union, for instance, has a greater degree of central authority than any other intergovernmental body. Transposing an EU-style project on the globe is unlikely in the near term, but a lot can be learned from past experience unless Europe is unique in world politics.

A host of "isms" have been proffered over the years to help explain integration in the European Union—functionalism, neo-functionalism, neo-neo-functionalism, liberal intergovernmentalism, and constructivism.[22] While Jan Zielonka and other pessimists predict a European unraveling and seek better theories of disintegration,[23] the EU has remained resilient in the face of crises. Hence, a more sensible objective is to understand the conditions under which the EU has thrived, especially if we hope to adapt elements of that experiment elsewhere. Given the EU's success, it is illogical to argue that supranationalism is hopelessly premature or utopian. Rather than a model to replicate, it is better to view the EU as a reflection of creative tensions between supranationalism and intergovernmentalism, a living laboratory for the possibilities of pushing out the envelope and expanding authority above national governments for the good of the whole.

Intergovernmental Organizations That Work

Norms and policies, as stated earlier, must find institutional homes if they are to avoid being ad hoc, episodic, idiosyncratic, and ultimately ineffective. Once adequate human and financial resources are allocated, an organization can be held accountable for performance; but even purportedly robust intergovernmental organizations often possess very inadequate wherewithal to attack the issues in their mandates. While throwing people and money at a problem does, of course, not guarantee success at the international any more than the national level, totally inadequate finances and minimal personnel with weak mandates and doubtful legitimacy often are at the heart of the explanation for the paucity of progress in the present world order.

The major disconnect in contemporary global governance is that the capacity to mobilize the resources—let alone muster the authority—to tackle global problems remains almost totally directed and controlled by states whereas problems are transnational. Our tools for making global policy—mainly state-to-state negotiations—are broken, leading to what Thomas Hale, David Held, and Kevin Young aptly called "gridlock."[24] This structural explanation for feeble intergovernmental organizations has elicited a host of proposals to provide more meaningful and independent resources—for example, by allocating a small tax levied on international airfares or financial transactions. However, member states insist on keeping the UN and other IGOs on as short a budgetary leash as possible to constrain their autonomy and ambitions.

EU finance ministers entertained a radical step by recommending in 2013 a so-called Robin Hood tax—modeled on the idea associated with the US Nobel laureate economist James Tobin. Their proposed levy would be small—one-tenth of a percentage point or less on the value of a trade—but it could earn billions of euros for humanitarian and environmental programs and struggling European governments. Such a proposal requires a political decision in Europe and comparable ones elsewhere. In particular, global problems require global institutional structures that have the scope and the capacity to attack them. More independence and initiative, not less, are desirable.

International institutions have been a target for my analytical energies over the last four decades. Some of my current research probes the origins of the United Nations during World War II as a serious war-fighting alliance *and* strategic commitment to multilateral cooperation. That is, it was not created as a liberal toy to be tossed aside when the going gets rough, but as a serious commitment to a longer-term strategy to foster peace and prosperity after the war.[25] Why do I bring up this history at this juncture? In *Requiem for a Nun*, William Faulkner provides the answer: "The past is not dead. It's not even past." E. H. Carr commented that history is an "unending dialogue between the past and the present."[26] The relevance of looking backward may not be immediately obvious to readers who are struggling with me to remove the question mark from "governing the world?" But it is pertinent for the authors of an international relations textbook who posit, "One of the often-perceived problems of the social sciences is their lack of historical depth."[27]

Having become a bit of a back-of-the-envelope historian over the last few decades, I struggle to remind myself and others of the extent to which current expectations for universal intergovernmental organizations are remarkably feeble in comparison with previous proposals from highly respected commentators. At Bretton Woods in 1944, for instance, John Maynard Keynes and the British delegation proposed a monetary fund equal to half of annual world imports while Harry Dexter White and the American side proposed a smaller fund of *only* one-sixth. One of the first economists recruited by the United Nations, Hans Singer, sardonically noted two decades ago, "Today's [International Monetary] Fund is only 2 per cent of annual world imports. Perhaps the difference between Keynes's originally proposed 50 percent and the actual 2 percent is a measure of the degree to which our vision of international economic management has shrunk."[28] The G20 decision in 2009 to alter IMF voting rules was a step toward "regime change" in that institution. Nonetheless, even after the 2009 infusion of close to $1 trillion during the financial crisis, the IMF still had one-twenty-fifth of the capital considered sensible by arguably the twentieth century's most able economist.

Furthermore, foes and some friends of the IMF regularly lambaste its excessive leverage resulting from the conditionality tied to loans. If so, what adjectives should we apply to capture the discrepancy between demonstrated and supposedly agreed needs and the actual wherewithal of such institutions as the Office of the High Commissioner for Human Rights and UNEP? If we had Keynes's or even White's expectations, imagine how cavernous the institutional gaps would be for human rights and the environment.

If international judicial proceedings are the way to foster greater respect for international law, a good thought experiment is to evaluate recent advances. The Security Council created ad hoc international criminal tribunals for the former Yugoslavia in 1993 and Rwanda in 1994 in order to seek justice against those responsible for war crimes, crimes against humanity, and genocide. In 2002 the council convened both a special court and a fact-finding commission in Sierra Leone. In 2003, it created a special court in East Timor and in 2005 established another hybrid court (part national and part international) in Cambodia to try members of the former Khmer Rouge regime who were responsible for the "killing fields." Perhaps the most ambitious attempt at international judicial proceedings is the International Criminal Court (ICC), based on the Rome Statute signed in 1998 that went into force in 2002. The ICC has begun to hand down judgments and has indicted Kenya's president and vice president elected in 2013. How substantial is the organizational shortfall when three permanent members of the Security Council—the United States, Russia, and China—have not yet ratified the treaty? Does their absence mean that the ICC is so weak as to be useless, or is it still helpful in building a viable legal edifice for global governance that might eventually tempt the dissenting major powers (as took place when the Security Council referred the Gaddhafi crew to the disputed court)?

In discussing the nature of the current array of intergovernmental organizations, reasonable people may disagree about the level of liquid in the global governance glass. We can debate the extent to which existing IGOs fall between those that work on at least certain issues at certain moments versus those that could be considered so weak as to constitute a virtual void even if well-appointed physical facilities and secretariats exist.

What is incontestable, however, is that most serious global threats encounter hesitant and insufficient progress toward ensuring compliance with agreed aims, and others do not even have those. Observers customarily shrug and point vaguely to insufficient political will as a catch-all explanation for failure. The lack of commitment and collective political spine is certainly a factor, but my argument is different. There is sufficient will to take modest steps toward filling knowledge, normative, and policy gaps, but states too rarely go the additional mile or kilometer to approve autonomous and fulsome international institutions to ensure cooperation and foster compliance. The existing array of such entities usually is sufficient to prevent total breakdown—for instance, in the 2008 financial meltdown—but inadequate to manage global problems. The planet will remain hard pressed to respond to current and future global challenges without more robust intergovernmental organizations, especially ones with universal membership.

Try as we might to airbrush the picture, the sum of IGOs in today's global governance is depressingly low—they are inadequately resourced and insufficiently empowered. And yet intergovernmental organizations that work and that are perceived as legitimate are a sine qua non for addressing virtually all global problems. "The time has come for the West to begin a fundamental rethink of its long-held policy," Kishore Mahbubani prescribes, "that it serves long-term Western interests to keep institutions of global governance weak."[29] His recommendation is spot-on but should apply to all other points on the world's political compass. The time has come to fundamentally rethink the long-held but myopic policy that weak IGOs somehow are in the interests of wealthy and poor countries alike, of governments and their citizens in the North and global South.

The playing field for global governance is changing, and new players are rushing to fill gaps identified by stakeholders and constituents. New organizations and new partnerships act to support governance of specific issues and respond to specific challenges. However, this improvised diversity has resulted in a complicated, weak, and inconsistent network of governance whereas solving global problems requires global norms, global law, and global buy-in. Depending on the issue area, geographic location, and time period, there are vast disparities in power and influence among states, IGOs, TNCs, and NGOs in the ways that they individually or collectively approach problem solving.[30] Sometimes global problems are flagged; sometimes they are discussed and recommendations agreed; but only occasionally are they even partially implemented. Consequently, today's world is governed by an indistinct and intricate patchwork of authority that is diffuse and contingent, creating inconsistent rules and varying degrees of effective collective action. It is better than nothing but totally inadequate.

One striking reason for inconsistent and ad hoc coverage is that IGOs are the weakest link in the chain binding together global governance. We would not expect the numbers of IGOs, especially those with universal membership, to increase the way that INGOs and TNCs have. Once there are institutions per sector and region, it is not additional numbers but additional resources and more robust mandates that are required. While sufficient in number—indeed, streamlining and consolidating are actually in order—most IGOs are simply without teeth. The growth in numbers of international organizations has been accounted for by private nonstate actors, whose dynamic increase has been coupled with more anemic growth in the activities and impact of intergovernmental institutions, both formal IGOs as well as their authority and accompanying public international law.

I have pointed to evidence of substantial change in the contemporary global governance landscape: One, new challenges to international peace and security and human survival have arisen. Two, new nonstate actors have appeared on the world stage, and some older ones have been transformed. Three, new norms and policies have proliferated. And four, new regional and global intergovernmental initiatives and institutions have resulted. At the same time, nothing has altered the fundamental validity of an evaluation over two decades ago by Adam Roberts and Benedict Kingsbury in *United Nations, Divided World*: "international society has been modified, but not totally transformed."[31]

Paradoxically, universal IGOs seem to be less central to foreign policies at exactly the moment when enhanced multilateralism is so desperately required.[32] As the authors of *Gridlock* indicate, on the "supply side ... institutionalized state cooperation has stalled."[33] The gap between the proliferation of and enthusiasm for NGOs and TNCs, on the one hand, and the dwindling interest in the actual activities and potential impact of universal IGOs, on the other hand, has serious implications for world order. Lacking the legal and hierarchical structures that such IGOs provide, ad hoc partnerships between public and private entities can only achieve so much. Without more formalized overarching structures, the impact of such partnerships will necessarily be uneven and far from optimal.

The plea for strengthened IGOs is not a surreptitious call for an all-powerful world government (or global tyrant) that would have frightened even Thomas Hobbes and made emperors jealous. According to Anne-Marie Slaughter, the glue binding the contemporary system of global governance is government networks, both horizontal and vertical.[34] Horizontal networks linking counterpart national officials across borders and through IGOs are one way to expand the reach of regulation, such as police investigators or financial regulators. Vertical networks are relationships between national officials and a supranational organization to which they have delegated authority, such as the European Court of Justice. In short, the relationship between national governments and IGOs does not go in one direction but rather reacts to pressures from many parties (e.g., lobbies and global civil society). Domestic and international politics have not been distinct but rather overlapping for some time, but now they have merged in many crucial respects. One solution for improving the punch of IGOs can come from strengthening existing networks and developing new ones.

But IGOs too should be substantially reformed and reinforced. While partnerships outside the state-based system are helpful, even essential, they also are unpredictable, episodic, and ultimately inadequate. Could multisector partnerships not be made far more effective within a more formal and regulated international system?

To return for a moment to the private sector's possible contributions to better global governance, we could illustrate the value-added of an IGO with an example of a self-regulatory governance system that can become wider practice, namely, the ad hoc adoption of systems for best-practice environmental management. While national and international regulation remains rudimentary and the need for more regulation hotly debated, many companies themselves have recognized environmentally sound activities as necessary—either due to public pressure or a perception that long-term sustainability is essential for a long-term business plan. Would it not be desirable to reinforce the bite of this recognition with overarching intergovernmental coordination? Would the spread of best practices then not be more rapid and learning more widespread?

Enter the International Standards Organization (ISO), one of the least well-known intergovernmental organizations composed of representatives from various national standard-setting organizations.[35] The ISO 14001 standard is a system designed to support the best practices of environmental impact by businesses and illustrates the kind of IGO value-added that we have in mind, in this case serving as the convener to bring together essential nonstate actors. IS0 14001 is based on actual performance, rather than some externally defined and arbitrary targets, and it is accepted because it is understood to work. In addition to identifying and spelling out specific internal controls for the management of environmental impact, ISO calls for certification of performance by such external actors as other private-sector firms or by third-party NGOs. That is, ISO 14001 operates not only to encourage good internal governance of TNC activities but also to stimulate TNCs to participate in international networks with other partners to improve governance. The spread of ISO 14001 illustrates not only complex interconnections among different actors in global governance but also the importance of state decisions in broadening the pool of TNCs interested in business to adopt these standards.[36]

The impression of vast and out-of-control bureaucracies in Brussels or New York is widespread and is a common complaint of ill-informed critics.

Maurice Bertrand—who evaluated UN practice and performance over two decades after having done so in France for a similar period—reminds us to keep in perspective the relative size and impact of all intergovernmental structures: "they are blamed for not doing what they are not given the means to do; faults that are often imaginary are ascribed to them, while their real faults go unnoticed; mythical explanations are invented to explain their ineffectiveness; and finally, there is very little recognition of the few significant results that they do achieve."[37]

All organizations—public and private, nonprofit or market-oriented—demonstrate pathologies and could be improved. Despite moaning and groaning from parliamentarians and taxpayers, we should keep in perspective the relative size of contemporary intergovernmental structures. The UN's annual core budget to administer an organization for the world is about the same as that of the City of New York's Fire Department; and the UN's record-breaking annual budgets in recent years for peace operations worldwide represent about a month's expenditures by the United States in Iraq before that war wound down.

Typically, IGOs are tarred and feathered for not doing what they are not given the means or authority to do. Kofi Annan used to joke that "SG" was not the abbreviation for "secretary-general" but "scape-goat." Imaginary faults are enumerated in detail. The needs for IGOs and their contributions, and especially their potential, are ignored.

Conclusion

Numerous examples of issue-specific global governance already exist—for instance, by the International Committee of the Red Cross for the laws of war and humanitarian principles,[38] the Fédération Internationale de Football Association (or FIFA, its familiar abbreviation) for the world's most popular sport (football or soccer), the International Association for Assigned Names and Numbers (also better known by its acronym, ICANN) for the Internet.[39] Corporations participate in novel governance arrangements such as the 1970s development of the Society for Worldwide Interbank Financial Telecommunication (SWIFT).[40]

Hence, multilevel governance—applying the notion of "subsidiarity" to accomplish tasks at the lowest level of authority that works, by a community group or a universal membership organization—is a reality that can and should be embraced and exploited to the maximum. Representatives of industry, NGOs, and multistakeholder coalitions sometimes determine policies and compliance as much as or more than many governments. Not-for-profit and for-profit nonstate actors play a crucial role in alleviating the lot of the poor, reducing greenhouse gases, investing in technologies, improving gender equality, and helping save lives.

However, something gets lost as we struggle to comprehend today's indistinct patchwork of authority and mosaic of old and new institutional structures interacting with an ever more complex web of local, national, bilateral, regional, and global processes and partnerships. Current intergovernmental organizations are insufficient in scope and ambition, inadequate in resources and reach, and not vested with the requisite authority; they lack competence and coordination capabilities; and they display incoherence in their policies and philosophies.

It is helpful to distinguish "hard" (formal organizations, treaties, and conventions) and "soft" (norms, principles, and practices) institutions. Governing the world requires both, which John Ruggie poetically describes as "what makes the world hang together."[41] I have argued that IGOs are unnecessarily marginal to our thinking exactly when more international collaboration, aided and abetted by them, is so sorely needed. This paradox coincides with another, namely, that we live in a period when globalization—and especially advances in information and communication technologies along with reduced barriers to transnational exchanges of goods, capital, services, people, ideas, and cultural influences—makes feasible something resembling intergovernmental organizations with at least some supranational characteristics. More robust global institutions are not only desirable but also feasible.

"To say the world is interdependent had become the worst kind of cliché," writes Kofi Annan in revisiting his decade at the helm of the UN. "True in the literal sense, but unable to generate the kinds of multilateral engagement befitting a world where no threat was limited to one country or region."[42] Uttering that the world is interdependent seemingly has become a substitute for action to generate the multilateral engagements required when more and more threats are not limited to one country or region.

While elements of global public goods can be provided regionally and by nonstate actors, there is no way around the cruel fact that their effective provision almost always requires considerable and worldwide multilateral coordination. Solving our governing-the-world puzzle requires that existing IGOs evolve. We do not really require more universal-membership global bodies—in fact, we could eliminate some and consolidate others—but rather a complete overhaul of those that exist. Additional resources and authority are necessary for universal-membership IGOs if we are to be more persuasive in asserting that it is possible for humanity to better govern the world.

Chapter Five
Beyond Platitudes

Addressing "Problems without Passports"

The lens of global governance expands our peripheral as well as in-depth vision. It allows us to see the fledgling steps that have already been taken to advance international order, predictability, stability, and fairness and to realize that we are not starting from scratch. In some ways many current global problems reflect, ironically in part, past successes with international cooperation—for instance, more states as a result of decolonization, more globalization as a result of trade liberalization, more institutions as a result of the processes of collaboration and specialization. We can observe the steady consolidation of the results, expectations, and rules in what Hedley Bull and his followers in the so-called English School call "international society"—perhaps more than he or we might have anticipated. One "exists when a group of states, conscious of certain common interests and common values, forms a society in the sense that they conceive themselves to be bound by a common set of rules in their relations with one another, and share in the working of common institutions."[1] Moreover, to the mix we add the energy, resources, and problem-solving skills of IGOs, NGOs, and TNCs—or "world society" in Barry Buzan's re-envisioning of the English School's approach to international society.[2] Peoples and transnational nonstate actors have mixed with states, or nonterritorial with territorial elements, in contemporary international relations.

We began by asking, is humanity collectively capable of "governing the world"? To a surprising extent, we have learned that we already do govern it. However, alongside the positive stories of collaborative networks, there are also demonstrable challenges in moving toward more effective global governance. To take one example, commerce transits the seas via container vessels with remarkable efficiency, a process that involves shippers, insurers, port authorities, labor unions, governments, and IGOs. But such global governance is hardly without its problems—oil spills, exploitation, and piracy to name a few. To take another example, the Kimberley Process was once much hailed as a multistakeholder solution to the problem of conflict minerals, but more recently it has been accused of ineffectiveness and an unwillingness to put in place adequate enforcement mechanisms.[3] Without more solid foundations in international law and without robust IGOs, global governance mechanisms are limited to voluntary participation, moral suasion, and peer pressure invoking democratic or market pressures in order to ensure compliance. The fledgling and inadequate contemporary structures of global governance must move beyond merely providing incentives for self-interested cooperation or problem solving à la carte.

Digging more deeply into many issues leads us to see dramatic flaws in the international system. In addition, too hastily affirming our collective abilities to govern the world would be ostrich-like and ahistorical. It would involve an unwarranted degree of self-satisfaction if we downplay existing and looming menaces to the world that we are seeking to govern better and overlook a landscape for policymaking and decision making that is fragmented to say the least. This book has used climate change to illustrate the point, but other examples include proliferation of WMDs (chemical, biological, and nuclear), pandemics, mass atrocities, cybercrime, global financial implosions, terrorism, poverty, and forced displacement. Readers surely can augment the list.

The proverbial bottom line is the following: Burgeoning actors and partnerships should certainly be acknowledged as a plus, but is what Tufts University blogger Daniel Drezner called "good enough" global governance[4] really good enough? The international system lacks central direction; it is constructed as much on the limited forms of governance produced by not-for-profit and for-profit nonstate actors as the tools accessible to govern-ments; it lacks a robust integration with the international legal system; and it certainly has no equivalent of the state's monopoly on the use of force. The world is not as unmoored as many pundits portray, but "better-than-nothing" global governance would be a more accurate description.

So where does that leave us? I do not intend to cast a pall of despair on the prospects for governing the world and addressing problems without passports but rather to suggest that a sober reading of the menaces facing the planet and the solutions currently being entertained should give pause. Indeed, in just over a decade we have lurched from crisis to crisis—9/11, the rise of new powers, the collapse of the world financial system, a threatened Eurozone, and unprecedented climate changes to name a few—which indicates clear fault lines and the need for adapting better our institutions to the global challenges staring us in the face.[5] Ad hoc approaches to problem solving simply cannot go on, and the persistent failures in handling the thorny problems resulting from environmental changes are exhibit A as to why we cannot merely muddle along, hoping somehow that we are drifting in the right direction.

The alternative is a three-pronged strategy that combines possible growth of various sorts: (1) the use of technologies—especially communication tech-nologies—to enhance accountability and assist in trustworthy negotiation; (2) market incentives for continued and expanded cooperation by stakeholders, especially in the private sector; and (3) wielding the power of states and of existing IGOs to mobilize and revamp their commitments to multilateralism.

We can better govern the world. We can address problems without pass-ports. Committed internationalists and citizens everywhere should pursue these three separate but complementary objectives. There is something here for everyone—father, mother, and child; CEO and custodian; overseas dip-lomat and community advocate. The mixture is, to use an expensive word, "polycentric" or anything but tidy—how else could it be in a world of mul-tiple and overlapping jurisdictions and allegiances, of cascading cultural and economic differences? "Variable geometry" is another.

This book is a modest effort to jump-start the task of understanding better the conditions under which the ways that the world is being governed can be improved. We need to maximize incentives and comparative advantages as part of pressuring ourselves and our governments to transform policy and action. And we need, in our own daily lives, to take small steps in the right collective direction—reducing, for instance, carbon footprints. But we also need to move beyond merely cobbling together occasional solutions.

So, should you be upbeat or depressed? My colleague, the distinguished historian David Nasaw, reminded me in one of my more despondent moments that the thirteen original colonies were waging the American Revolution under the weak and contested Articles of Confederation. However, in 1787 they sought a "more perfect union" in Philadelphia. The weak confederation of 193 UN member states—the original 1946 General Assembly had 51, but decolonization and the aftermath of the Cold War have added another 142—requires a "Philadelphia moment,"[6] one that is informed by the reality of contemporary global governance. Undoubtedly, such a moment for the world will require time to gestate—the United States in the eighteenth century had the advantage of being a sparsely populated territory inhabited by people with a common culture and language, and the world is much more complex. We can, however, move toward a comparable global arrangement (also present in such other countries as Switzerland) in which the center respects the autonomy of the periphery, in which the center takes care not to abuse its power.

In terms of the three-pronged future strategy, the first prong—the enlarged use of the political and economic possibilities opened by the communications revolution that began late in the twentieth century—offers huge opportunities but is beyond the scope of this short volume. However, the other two elements of the strategy loom large and are topics that have preoccupied me for years. They involve more concrete institutional designs and provide the conclusion: market incentives for multisector partnerships to expand the formidable practical global governance that already exists; and harnessing and revitalizing the power of the state and current IGOs, most especially those of the UN system.

Multisector Partnerships

The growth of nonstate actors has meant a diversity of potential players and partners active on the world's stage. Their presence and activities have broken new ground on which new architectures of global governance with multisector partnerships have been and can be built. Such partnerships represent a new way to govern the world as these pages have made clear, albeit one that is underresearched and poorly understood, especially the role of transnational business.

The widespread recognition of the growing traction of nonstate actors is essential because they not only represent stakeholders but also contribute concretely to contemporary global problem solving. As such, we have moved a long distance from the state-centric model of traditional international relations. The proliferation of nonstate actors has ushered in an age of global partnerships between private and public bodies on numerous specific issues. Multisector partnerships are a valuable addition to the international toolkit even if their limitations are clear. A few examples from today's script for global governance hint at the complex interactions among states, IGOs, and nonstate actors of various stripes; they should help dramatically make the point that these partnerships make a difference.

Over the last decade, some 100,000 international peacekeepers (soldiers, police, and civilian monitors) have been deployed annually worldwide in war zones. Such personnel on the ground have come from the UN and such regional organizations as the African Union or subregional ones as the Economic Community of West African States, alliances such as NATO, coalitions of the willing, or some combination of the above.[7] Alongside states and IGO-mandated troops, a host of not-for-profit humanitarian and development agencies funded by states, foundations, and direct public donations worked in war-torn areas and fragile states to save lives and support economic development and provide public goods such as health care, education, and access to clean water. In addition, local and international for-profit companies operated in countries before, during, and after armed conflicts.

Countering threats posed by transnational criminal networks demands collective action across borders. Interrupting terrorist designs on subways in London and Tokyo or airports in Jeddah and Kuala Lumpur requires inputs from several countries and from the International Criminal Police Organization (better known as "Interpol"), as does countering narcotics- and human-trafficking rings. Halting money laundering requires cooperation by banks and regulators worldwide.[8] And counter-piracy efforts off the horn of

Africa would not be as effective without the shipping industry's participation in the Contact Group on Piracy off the Coast of Somalia, a multistakeholder mechanism that includes governments, UN agencies, and nonstate actors.

Since the collapse of the Seattle WTO meeting in 1999, the changing sources available for development have dampened protests and elevated the perceived importance of trade's benefits for sustainable growth.[9] Meanwhile in poorer countries, remittances from migrant workers and foreign direct investment have come to dwarf charitable funds and grants from the dwindling (in percentage terms) flow of official development assistance. Indeed, remittances from the African diaspora alone in 2010 (the latest year for which World Bank figures are available) were about $50 billion whereas official development assistance was about $10 billion less.[10] As state-based systems struggle to support economic development, nonstate resources have played a substantial role. For example, support for public health coming from the Gates Foundation has become more significant than that from the World Health Organization; and some pharmaceutical companies have provided substantial low-cost drugs to alleviate the AIDS epidemic.[11] Countless nonprofit organizations have worked within various partnerships within all sectors of development cooperation.

These illustrations describe situations in which a variety of actors came together in different combinations and different intensities to address specific problems, with varying degrees of success. In doing so, states and nonstates cobbled together a framework for cooperation; and many of the responses have resulted in more order, stability, and predictability than many might have expected from looking at an organizational chart for the world. In short, they have contributed to improving global governance, which goes far beyond a system of coordination by state-based entities to embrace multisector partnerships.

State-centric structures—states themselves and their creations in the form of IGOs—no longer enjoy a monopoly or even oligopoly over collective efforts to improve international society and world order. Hybrid global governance arrangements are increasingly prevalent; and they are not merely facilitators or epiphenomena of globalization. Neither of these claims is difficult to support.

That states are no longer the sole—or in some instances the most crucial—actors in parts of the existing world order has long been a preoccupation for researchers. The ever more crowded governance stage means that "states' ability to control or regulate [global economic growth] has diminished, while nonstate actors' efforts to shape or tame it have increased."[12] Peter Willetts has pointed out that nonstate actors have not only participated in global governance but also been involved in its construction.[13] The third wave of democratization certainly has speeded the growth of nonstate actors in global governance, which in turn has supported networks of various types to foster additional transnational interactions.

Society—local, national, international, and world—is too complex for citizens' demands to be satisfied by governments alone. Civil society organizations play active roles in shaping norms, laws, and policies. They provide additional pathways and levers for people and all levels of government to improve the effectiveness and enhance the legitimacy of public policy at all levels of governance. They challenge traditional notions of representation, accountability, and legitimacy. Similarly, for-profit corporations expand their purview beyond mere bottom lines to delve into arenas (active participation in international conferences, for example) and activities (corporate social responsibility, for example) that formerly were either absent or peripheral.[14] In an increasingly diverse, complex, and interdependent world, states alone cannot address societal needs; they cannot pretend to have all the answers for collective action or most other questions

One key illustration of the changing structure of actors engaged in transnational activities was the establishment of the UN Global Compact (UNGC) at the Millennium Summit of 2000, an initiative aimed at encouraging corporate participation in the protection of human rights and sustainable development and at involving NGOs in monitoring TNC performance.[15] The United Nations, the foremost IGO and preeminent global governance institution, finally was obliged to acknowledge the existence of members of the private sector—both the for-profit and nonprofit species—as essential partners in supporting UN goals and decisions. More recently, the UN secretary-general's High-Level Panel of Eminent Persons on the Post-2015 Development Agenda coined "global partnership" to capture the reality that progress on development, like every other sector, will involve not just governments but also business, civil society, and individuals.[16] Still more recently the Oxford Martin Commission for Future Generations recommended greater use of "creative coalitions" to capture the need to resort to ad hoc groups spanning governments, IGOs, NGOs, foundations, and business.[17]

In short and as stressed earlier, the world organization has ceased being essentially an exclusive club of governments. In fact, calling the UN an "intergovernmental organization" is somewhat misleading in that what was predominantly the "first UN" of member states has always been backed by what Inis Claude called the "second UN" (of international civil servants).[18] But over several decades, a prominent new phenomenon has become far less peripheral and more essential—namely, the "third UN" of experts, commissions, NGOs, TNCs, and interested individuals.[19] Although in an IGO like the United Nations states pay the bills and make decisions within the intergovernmental arena, to be meaningful UN actions have to be implemented by staff members and increasingly have to embrace nonstate actors as well. In some ways, the UN can be viewed as both a state and a nonstate actor.

The "messiness," or complexity, of the image of "three UNs" is a microcosm of global governance more generally. In reflecting upon the turn of the century and the missing "third UN" of both civil society and business, Kofi Annan recalls, "I was convinced that the UN would achieve little in the 21st century unless it reached out to such people and convinced them that it was a useful ally, able and willing to work with them to achieve their ends."[20] In fact, until the end of the Cold War, the for-profit private sector was virtually absent from UN corridors and deliberations because of the ideological biases in socialist countries and much of the Third World. But the Global Compact altered that situation and was a specific recognition of the crucial role of TNCs. The data on its membership since 2000 demonstrate a steady increase of companies committed to respecting its terms and conditions. Although the time elapsed is shorter, of the 7,259 companies represented as members in the UNGC in 2012, almost 80 percent had joined since 2006 and almost half (44.5 percent) in the previous two years. As with the growth of IGOs and NGOs, the growth rate of corporate participation in global networks appears to have developed steadily and accelerated until the aftermath of the global financial crisis.

The UNGC demonstrates that these ever-evolving systems represent new mechanisms for global governance. The Global Compact asks TNCs to voluntarily commit to principles supporting sustainable business practices, which then are supposed to be carried out throughout the structures of participating companies. Performance is monitored by still other nonstate partners, participating NGOs. Rather than seeking compliance through punitive sanctions, appropriate conduct is sought through voluntary-based initiatives; and actors adhere because their reputations are on the line. Abraham and Antonia Chayes argued two decades ago that such norm diffusion and incentives can be more powerful mechanisms for changing behavior than penalties.[21] In doing so, the compact's members set policies that govern their own activities and those of their subsidiaries and suppliers. Given the size and impact of the most powerful TNCs, this effort to improve governance is not trivial: TNC policies and procedures can have a direct impact on the health, education, and well-being of the individuals who work for them. They can help to bring employees in line with international standards for professionalism or technical proficiency through training and furnishing illustrative cases that demonstrate the utility of these practices.[22] In addition, the impact of these policies has significant ripple effects on other institutions; work by Chuck Kwok and Solomon Tadesse, for example, has found that TNC activities that incorporate deliberate refusals to engage in corruption can actively reduce that blight in host states.[23]

Although modern multistakeholder networks lack any formal legal authority and may come and go, they can nonetheless shape collective responses in ways that have a meaningful impact on global problem solving. The typical abilities of national governments to provide security, development, and access to other public goods are enhanced by partnering with nonstate actors.

The State: Distinguishing Bathwater and Baby

Nothing written here should shroud the state's centrality for national, regional, and global problem solving. The growing salience of nonstate actors means a lot of things, but it does not mean tossing out the state. At the same time, states and their creations, the current generation of IGOs, cannot by themselves address many actual and likely global problems. While improvements are plausible and highly desirable today within the decentralized system of global governance, we need substantially more empowered

IGOs; and tomorrow states will have to use the authority vested in them by their citizens to commit to rebuilding more authoritative intergovernmental organizations, especially those with universal membership in the UN system.

These pages have also documented a breathless pace of change in the international system. One of the more dramatic alterations in great-power perspectives, for instance, resulted in the shift from the G5/7/8 to the G20, an indication from leading states that they had to yield some elements of their privileges to guarantee greater inclusion of the world's emerging economies.[24] The result was a greater buy-in from more states into a particular form of problem solving at the global level. But this clear recognition that more support from, collaboration with, and cost sharing by other key states should not be confused with transformation. We require more than slow and marginal adaptations to help cope with and manage the constraints working against vigorous collective action within the existing international system. While gradual change in decision-making procedures and judicial interpretations helped move the European Coal and Steel Community to the European Economic Community to the European Union, the pressures of time alone from several looming global threats would argue for picking up the pace. Tinkering will not suffice, especially as it often is a stalling device rather than a step toward an alternative vision.

Whatever we think of its current impact, fundamentally the current system of global governance is a second- or third-best surrogate for authority and enforcement. However useful to explain complex multilateral and transboundary phenomena as well as collaborative efforts, it lacks prescriptive power. We are obliged to ask whether global *governance*, no matter how improved, can address the full range of global menaces if it lacks the elements of global *government*.

The idea of a global government has a long history. International relations specialists previously interpreted advances in international organization and law not simply as moves in the right direction and more effective than unilateral efforts and the law of the jungle. But they also observed the march of history and foresaw a growing web of IGOs and public international law as helpful in a stumbling yet steady and inexorable progression toward authoritative arrangements for the world. Paradoxically when states actually could address or attenuate most problems for their own populations, the idea of world government remained an imaginable scenario, even if it was a mostly fringe notion. Now, when states visibly cannot tackle an ever-growing number of threats, world government is considered unimaginable, completely beyond the pale. Many observers even look askance upon the idea of more muscular intergovernmental organizations.

Another important change in thinking about global government is that earlier conceptual efforts emphasized the state and only grudgingly admitted the capabilities of other actors, in particular IGOs. Now that both civil society and market-oriented groups have joined the fray of international problem solving, we risk going too far in the other direction, overestimating the capabilities of for-profit groups and NGOs and underestimating the importance of IGOs. Burgeoning numbers of NGOs and TNCs have resources and energy, to be sure, but we should not go overboard in our enthusiasm. More robust IGOs are still a crucial piece of the puzzle in a world so obviously lacking in machinery to address the problems inherent in globalization, to deal adequately with most of the life-threatening challenges that already exist or soon will. Local and national jurisdictions remain crucial for local and national problem solving, but global problems require global solutions. Nonstate actors—norm entrepreneurs, activists crossing borders, epistemic communities, profit-seeking corporations, and transnational social networks—can make and have made important and even essential contributions to better global governance; but they cannot eliminate poverty, fix climate change, ensure macroeconomic stability, agree on international standards, or halt mass atrocities. Such polycentric approaches can even exacerbate fragmentation and be considered a sleight-of-hand and distraction in that they cannot in isolation fill global governance gaps. While decentralized institutional innovations give the impression of movement in the right direction, merely increasing the number and diversity of actors could, in fact, be counterproductive. It is not more voices but what they say that matters. The-more-the-merrier provides a poor policy guide; rather, we should be heralding the-better-and-the-more-coherent-the-merrier.

The downside to date of global governance is mindlessly applauding the creation of what amounts to a "Global Tea Party." While the private can complement the public sector and be an essential partner, the private simply cannot do everything better than the public sector. Mini- and multi-multilateralisms are positive developments, but their limitations should be obvious as well. More NGOs and TNCs are hardly a panacea. Without more robust IGOs (especially universal ones) and elements of supranational regulatory power, states and their citizens will not reap the benefits of trade and globalization, discover nonviolent ways to settle disputes, or address environmental deterioration.

In *The Structure of Scientific Revolutions*, Thomas Kuhn famously outlined how a dominant paradigm—or "way of seeing the world"—is replaced. Shortcomings in a worldview become clear when puzzling anomalies (or things that make no sense) require alternative explanations. If too many anomalies and auxiliary hypotheses result, a new paradigm is required because "the anomalous has become the expected."[25] Kuhn's classic example was the shift from Ptolemy's model of planets rotating around a fixed Earth when that orthodoxy simply could no longer explain observations made with new instruments (the telescope especially) or predict what was going to happen.

We have not arrived there for state sovereignty. The Copernican moment is not yet upon us because the anarchy of which realist theorists and many government officials are so fond still predicts much but certainly not all of international relations. If anarchy is equated with the absence of central authority for the world, that definition still holds. Nonetheless, other elements of the classic definition have far less explanatory value than even a few decades ago, and certainly it makes no sense, despite the resilience of great power politics, to analyze international relations through the lens of a unitary state acting alone and with complete autonomy. Hence, we should emulate a young Copernicus; we should stare at the sun and planets at which others have been gazing for three and a half centuries but articulate alternative views for the relations among them. We can point to the obvious (to me at least) reality that sovereign states remain the foundation of the contemporary world order, but they no longer are unquestioned authorities, too rarely provide public goods, and increasingly are unable to solve global problems crying out for solutions.

Kal Holsti's *Taming the Sovereigns* probes the concept of change and ways of measuring it. He points out that change is quite different for someone playing today's stock market and for those of us trying to understand it in international relations, where recent events are not of interest unless they have a demonstrable effect on how diplomatic, military, economic, political, or humanitarian work is actually done. He notes, "This is the Hegelian and

Marxist problem: at what point does quantitative change lead to qualitative consequences?"[26] In other words, we can also characterize as "new" a tipping point at which quantitative change is so substantial that it constitutes something qualitatively "new."

In the end, I do not expect to settle grand debates about change versus continuity. There is always a bit of both. However, we are approaching a transitional moment, an interlude signaling a possible tectonic shift in the way that we govern the world. I remain an inveterate optimist: human beings can organize themselves to address and attenuate the global problems that we and our ancestors have created. The image of a "global village" has been overused because not all problems are global. But for those that are—and an increasing number are no longer abstract specters but staring us in the face—we indeed inhabit a global village. Transformative institutional developments should be at least in our thinking and not far beyond the horizon.

The extant world order cannot survive in its present form. Hopefully wisdom and insight can catalyze a paradigm change, and we are not obliged to await more crises and catastrophes. But will the leaders of states—the "village elders" so to speak—be wise enough to avoid tragedies as seemingly the only catalysts for change?

The Path Ahead

Sovereign entities are, like other formerly dominant rulers, oblivious to their weaknesses and decline. Their defensiveness of sacrosanct sovereignty in diplomatic settings is reminiscent of Shakespeare because it is fair to say that states "doth protest too much, methinks."[27] Politicians and diplomats should also be obliged to read Percy Bysshe Shelley's "Ozymandias":

> And on the pedestal these words appear:
> "My name is Ozymandias, king of kings:
> Look on my works, ye Mighty and despair!"
> Nothing beside remains. Round the decay
> Of that colossal wreck, boundless and bare
> The lone and level sands stretch far away.

As long as I am asking politicians and diplomats to read poetry, I might as well propose that the rest of us adopt a new global anthem. Along with Billie Holiday, we can sing "Crazy He Calls Me," whose lyrics resonate: "The difficult I'll do right now. The impossible will take a little while."

We should recall that both Hans Morgenthau and the theologian Reinhold Niebuhr had concluded by the 1960s that a world state was necessary because of the existence of nuclear weapons.[28] Realism's father, E. H. Carr, warned readers in the interwar years that tempering utopia with power, and vice versa, was necessary to avoid despair and stagnation in thinking.[29] He was preoccupied not only about international legalism and the realities of power but also about unbridled power without a moral compass. In other words, the midwives of realism did not exclude a global government and understood that a vision, however seemingly quixotic, of where we should be headed was necessary to avoid getting mired in the present and going nowhere. Disillusionment is a dead-end street. Oscar Wilde, in "The Soul of Man under Socialism," described this insight more crisply: "A map of the world that does not include Utopia is not worth looking at."[30]

Wishing does not constitute a viable strategy, of course, which necessitates more than a dollop of both power and incentives in our analytical thinking. More specifically, it requires addressing the possibilities for the erosion of state sovereignty, intensifying solidarity and fairness, and establishing IGOs that are up to the tasks of the twenty-first century.

No one really knows what the future holds. Without a long-term vision, however, we are obliged to accept the contours of our unacceptable world order, including the feeble organizations that constitute the contemporary UN system.[31] Social scientists resemble politicians and customarily are 180 degrees away from forward thinking most of the time. We focus on today and maybe next month; the long term consists of the next election cycle. Yet Andrew Hurrell usefully reminds us about the "relentless presentism" that afflicts political science and international relations.[32] His concern was ignoring the past in understanding the present, a preoccupation that I share; but not moving out in time and ignoring the possibilities for future world orders also is a mammoth constraint of presentism.

While federalism means many things to many people, fundamentally it aims to acknowledge, preserve, and accommodate diverse identities, interests, and cultures. A workable future design for the planet is not yet formed because no federal state is identical to any other. Each incorporates and accommodates differences via formal constitutional means that adjust and adapt to changing circumstances. The one for the world will require imagination and tenacity to capture a global pluralist order that could hardly be more complex. At the very least, we should begin a conversation, which has been absent since the 1930s or 1940s, about an idea that has descended into the doldrums and desuetude. The ultimate objective of any overarching authority for the world would be integration and not assimilation. The planet, like the European Union, requires a strong but restricted central authority that accommodates as much local diversity and initiative as possible.

Struggling with where ideally we should be headed and formulating how we could get there are prerequisites to avoid going nowhere, or perhaps even moving backward. The Quaker economist Kenneth Boulding repeated often, "We are where we are because we got there."[33] His insight was also, of course, that we can go where we need to go by getting there. The first step is imagining what that more desirable order looks like, the second is formulating how we could move toward it, and the third is taking action.

It is ironic that even the most committed internationalists no longer dare imagine what is required beyond tinkering. Most countries, and especially the major powers, are very distant indeed from accepting elements of an overarching authority and the accompanying inroads on national autonomy. As corny as it sounds at the moment, however, global federalism will not seem so far-fetched a half century from now—just as an integrated, peaceful, and prosperous Europe appeared perfectly preposterous amid the ashes of World War II.

It is problematic to apply lessons across geographical divides—Europe's common cultural heritage, common history, and anchoring in a common Judeo-Christian culture may seem especially incongruous for a planet with few characteristics that could be preceded by the adjective "common." Yet there also was no historical precedent for the European Union. Pooling sovereignty in specific historical circumstances holds lessons because institutions are not merely tools of their creators but can take on lives of their own. In attempting to find ways to govern the world, the question is whether collectively we are stumbling as Europe was in 1945 when it began moving in another direction.

"Surviving the war was one thing," is how historian Tony Judt characterized that moment; "surviving the peace was another."[34]

An arguably unwarranted degree of speculation and jitters about the EU's future have accompanied the gloom between the 2009 Greek and 2013 Cyprus debt crises; record unemployment there and in Spain, Portugal, and Italy; as well as the return of virulent Euro-skepticism from the far-right led by the United Kingdom Independence Party, Marine Le Pen's National Front in France, and Geert Wilders's Freedom Party in the Netherlands. In economic tough times, disillusionment is quick to appear. Brussels provides a convenient scapegoat, an easy target for many people as the cause of their mounting troubles rather than as a way to get them out of the current mess. Europe's citizens could certainly forget the distance traveled from the moment described by Judt and oppose the transfer of more power to EU institutions, which European Council president Herman Van Rompuy recognized when accepting the 2012 Nobel Peace Prize. He poignantly dredged up and repeated Abraham Lincoln's sobering words: "What is being assessed today is whether that union, or any union so conceived and so dedicated, can long endure." The fact that the heads of three of the EU's major institutions—the Commission, the Council, the Parliament—collected the prize together symbolized the lack of institutional clarity that is the EU's core problem at present.[35]

Yet the European experiment will endure as the American one has. Observers focus on the "remaining superpower" (the United States) or the "emerging superpower" (China), somehow overlooking the European Union as what Andrew Moravcsik aptly describes the "second superpower."[36] The combined GDP of the twenty-eight EU members is larger than that of the United States; its trade with both the United States and with China is greater than either of those countries with each other; and EU countries account for half of global foreign aid and a quarter of military expenditures. Even those who see my interpretation as too rosy—who like Simon Hix are concerned by policy gridlock in Brussels, the lack of citizen engagement, and the specter of un-governability—judge the EU to be a "remarkable achievement."[37] With some luck over the next few decades—undoubtedly punctuated by the ups and downs that have always accompanied historically important experiments—the world collectively could be where Europe was in the early 1950s, struggling under conditions of anarchy to cooperate before groping to find ways to collaborate and then identifying ways to integrate and pursue common purposes.

Moving deliberately but with some urgency would reflect Jean Monnet's modernist convictions about a political strategy of small, concrete steps.[38] European states wisely rejected a more draconian "big bang" approach from Altiero Spinelli, who proposed starting with ambitious political institutions and a popularly endorsed treaty that quickly would have been translated into a constitution for a federal state.[39] Rather than being overly ambitious—that is, aiming for universal participation on all issues—the EU experience indicates that "a better approach is to encourage nations to submit to a higher authority *in those areas where they are prepared to do so.*"[40]

Ironically, the continent that gave birth to the current international system could act as a catalyst for a post-Westphalian one with more cosmopolitan multilateralism. Driven largely by the forces of globalization, the contemporary system of global governance is being transformed, not by replacing states but rather by extending their boundaries to encompass new issues and new actors. This postmodern and nonterritorial overlay of global governance is characterized by an extensive transnationalization of issues, exchanges, and actors that blurs boundaries and intermingles public and private, civic and market.

If limited sharing results in improved security and prosperity, stranger things have happened than the creation of a sovereignty-sharing global organization. I am not tilting at windmills. I am not refurbishing moth-eaten ideas. As the economist and philosopher Albert Hirschman quipped, "History is nothing if not far-fetched."[41]

Most reasonable individuals agree to voluntarily limit their personal rights in order to enjoy a secure and prosperous community; this fact is the "social contract" or bargain struck to avoid the "solitary, poor, nasty, brutish, and short" lives in Thomas Hobbes's "state of nature."[42] The revival of political cosmopolitanism challenges the deeply ingrained presupposition that the primary and only site for identity is the state.[43] Opponents of world government worry about an overwhelming tyranny, but such European theorists of cosmopolitan democracy as Daniele Archibugi and David Held urge us to remember that a central state is not the only variant for transnational order, that other types of imagined communities can be viable.[44]

The tonic is moving toward a multilayered, minimal world authority based on the principles of federalism and subsidiarity with networks of actors still having incentives to act productively in arenas where they have a comparative advantage. Ours is a period of economic turmoil, ideological confusion, and organizational flux. A world in transition and changing rapidly on so many fronts makes shared appreciations tough and collective action elusive. The *Human Development Report 2013* employs "collective pluralism" to describe the challenges ahead in the midst of fledgling and often confusing efforts to empower institutions at all levels to work in a more coordinated and complementary fashion. Almost two decades ago, the Carnegie Endowment's Jessica Mathews foresaw such messy governance arrangements as "the new medievalism," referring to a variety of organizational units and authorities (states, nonstates, markets) operating without a clear center or hierarchy, resembling the dynamics of the Middle Ages.[45] While loosely knit networks of institutions provide some of the in-depth expertise and flexibility necessary to address diverse challenges faced by the planet, effective action is also tougher with so much institutional fragmentation. Competition and turf battles, communications problems, redundancy, and pathologies add to an already terrifying level of complexity in problem solving.

It is hard to visualize a better organized system of multilayered global governance built on unprecedented levels of dispersed authority, but this alternative is more viable than an easy-to-caricature World Leviathan. A stark, binary cleavage between global governance and global government suggests a larger chasm between the two that is neither necessary nor justified. We have examined the growth of networks in not-for-profit and market-oriented nonstate actors as healthy inputs that augment the current capacity of the international system to provide some government-like services for the planet. But why are more robust universal-membership intergovernmental organizations a bridge too far?

International order has been built and rebuilt on numerous occasions; and yesterday's institutions often are ill equipped to tackle today's problems. The question is whether a third generation of multilateral organizations will arise quickly and as a result of unnecessary and unspeakable tragedies—as earlier crisis innovations like the League of Nations or the United Nations arose phoenix-like from the ashes of the twentieth century's world wars and the Congress of Vienna from the Napoleonic wars—or more deliberately founded on the evolutionary potential of constructing an edifice on the basis of more modest functional bases. Contemplating the former option is not soothing even if history informs us that such tragedies are the customary currency for global institutional reforms. This optimist is betting on the human capacity for learning and adapting to prevent suffering on a scale that could well dwarf the twentieth century's wars. "Whether our accumulated connectivity and experience has created fresh perspectives on global governance and an ability to transcend national orders," Ian Goldin cautions, "remains the most critical question of our time."[46]

The crying need for intergovernmental organizations with teeth is too often shortchanged in thinking about problem solving. Perhaps they have always been too few in number and arrived too late on the scene and with too little punch. But in the second decade of the twenty-first century, addressing our collective problems requires, at a minimum, building more robust IGOs, especially the UN system but at the regional level as well, with wider scope and more resources.

Why? The market simply will not graciously provide solutions to ensure human survival with dignity. The menaces described earlier are not remote but for the here and now. As Thomas Hale, David Held, and Kevin Young remind us, "demand for international cooperation is growing even as supply grinds to a halt."[47] Adam Smith's "invisible hand" operates even less well among states to solve transboundary problems than it does within states to solve domestic ones. There are limits to volunteers beyond borders, the main recruiting device for staffing global governance today. The adaptability and flexibility of global governance is a hallmark and a genuine strength, but the various combinations of partnerships also face severe limitations. The supply of global public goods lags far behind today's demands, and tomorrow's requirements will be even more sobering. Unadulterated state sovereignty implies the voluntary supply of such goods. We have encountered examples of discretionary global governance, but we need to accelerate the pace, to move beyond occasionally doing the right thing but usually doing too little too late.

Mid-2013 scientific measurements indicated CO_2 levels had reached 400 parts per million, a level of poison that the best available evidence suggests had not been present for 3 million years. Useful counsel comes from an unlikely source, four Republicans who are former administrators of the US Environmental Protection Agency: "When confronted by a problem, deal with it. Look at the facts, cut through the extraneous, devise a workable solution and get it done."[48] Decades of efforts to bring emissions under control clearly are faltering. The late Donella Meadows, the American environmentalist who did so much to launch and sustain debate including her weekly column "The Global Citizen," is widely reported to have responded regularly and routinely when asked if it was too late to do anything about climate change and other global challenges: "We have exactly enough time—starting now."[49]

Conclusion

I reiterate in closing that states are and will remain the fundamental building blocks for a system of governing the world even if we take maximum advantage of the energy, resources, and skills of nonterritorial actors. However, "bringing the state back in," as a celebrated academic title put it,[50] is cute but empirically inaccurate. States never left, except in a few imaginations, and will not depart any time soon. Yet outdated international relations theory goes far beyond this reality and posits states as essential and nonstate actors as peripheral. Substantially modifying that atavistic and antiquated view does not mean that national, regional, and global problems can be addressed without states. However, states and IGOs will not be able to counter today's, let alone tomorrow's, catastrophes even when supplemented by the energy, resources, and problem-solving skills of nonstate actors. The world is far more crowded and connected than the one in which the current generation of multilateral organizations was created; and these ossified structures have not kept up with the pace of emerging problems and are losing the battle to address those for which boundaries are irrelevant.

An illustration of why global problems require global cooperation—and why it can work—is evident from the discovery of the Higgs boson particle by the European Organization for Nuclear Research (CERN) in 2012. The director of CERN announced, "It is a global effort, it was a global effort, and it's a global success."[51] Fifty years of theorizing and experimentation—that is, decades of coordinated intellectual and scientific collaboration—required the work of thousands of scientists and institutes and investments from member countries over multiyear periods: in short, global cooperation through an intergovernmental organization that works.

H. G. Wells in *The Shape of Things to Come* called world government "manifestly the only possible solution of the human problem."[52] His fantasy overstated the case in 1933, but his proposition has more resonance today. No matter how muscular the inputs from informal and formal networks, no matter how copious the resources from private foundations and corporations, no matter how much goodwill from individuals and governments, we cannot continue to ignore and rationalize the absence of overarching authority. Continued advances in global governance are desirable, feasible, and beneficial. But we are obliged to honestly ask, as the introduction did, is adequate, let alone good, global governance imaginable without world government? No. It is time we opened our minds and consider all of the ways that we might best govern the world. We can address pesky problems without passports. Humanity collectively is capable of better and more fairly governing the world.

Notes

Introduction

1. Mark Mazower, *Governing the World: The History of an Idea* (New York: Penguin, 2012), 427. After this manuscript went to press, I discovered an intriguing set of essays assembled by two talented younger analysts who also trace how contemporary governance works: Sophie Harman and David Williams, eds., *Governing the World? Cases in Global Governance* (London: Routledge, 2013).

2. Harold K. Jacobson, *Networks of Interdependence: International Organizations and the Global Political System*, 2nd ed. (New York: Knopf, 1984), 84.

3. Charles Darwin, *The Descent of Man and Selection in Relation to Sex* (New York: Appleton and Co., 1897), 122.

4. Kofi A. Annan, "What Is the International Community? Problems without Passports," *Foreign Policy*, no. 132 (Sept.–Oct. 2002): 30–31.

5. Thomas G. Weiss and Ramesh Thakur, *Global Governance and the UN: An Unfinished Journey* (Bloomington: Indiana University Press, 2010).

Chapter One

1. Michael Barnett and Raymond Duvall, "Introduction," in *Power in Global Governance,* ed. Michael Barnett and Raymond Duvall (Cambridge: Cambridge University Press, 2005), 1.

2. Derek Heater, *World Citizenship and Government: Cosmopolitan Ideas in the History of Western Political Thought* (New York: St. Martin's Press, 1996).

3. Richard B. Falk and Saul H. Mendlovitz, eds., *A Strategy of World Order*, volumes I–IV (New York: World Law Fund, 1966–1967); and Grenville Clark and Louis B. Sohn, *World Peace through World Law* (Cambridge, MA: Harvard University Press, 1958).

4. Charles Krauthammer, "The Unipolar Moment," *Foreign Affairs* 70, no. 1 (1990–91): 23–33.

5. James N. Rosenau and Ernst Czempiel, eds., *Governance without Government: Order and Change in World Politics* (Cambridge: Cambridge University Press, 1992).

6. Commission on Global Governance, *Our Global Neighbourhood* (Oxford: Oxford University Press, 1995).

7. Following World War II, the World Peace Foundation started and subsidized the journal *International Organization*, which had ceased to examine what its title promised. "From the late 1960s, the idea of international organization fell into disuse," Timothy Sinclair reminds us. "*International Organization*, the journal which carried this name founded in the 1940s, increasingly drew back from matters of international policy and instead became a vehicle for the development of rigorous academic theorizing" (Timothy J. Sinclair, *Global Governance* [Cambridge, UK: Polity Press, 2012], 16). Rather than a publication on the desks of practitioners, *International Organization* had become esoteric scholarly fare with an editorial board and authors who too rarely set foot in the real world of policy, who sought rewards in abstraction, not action.

8. Lawrence Finkelstein, "What Is Global Governance?" *Global Governance* 1, no. 3 (1995): 368.

9. Thomas G. Weiss and Rorden Wilkinson, "Rethinking Global Governance: Complexity, Authority, Power, Change," *International Studies Quarterly* 58, no. 2 (2014): forthcoming. See also Thomas G. Weiss and Rorden Wilkinson, "Global Governance to the Rescue: Saving International Relations?" *Global Governance* 20, no. 1 (2014): forthcoming.

10. The connotations in Latin (and its Greek etymological predecessor, *kubernán*) are helpful here. See Anne Mette Kjaer, *Governance* (Cambridge, UK: Polity Press, 2004), 3.

11. Scott Barrett, *Why Cooperate? The Incentive to Supply Global Public Goods* (Oxford: Oxford University Press, 2007), 19.

12. William James, *Pragmatism and Other Writings* (New York: Penguin, 2000 [1907]), 88.

13. Michael Barnett, *Empire of Humanity: A History of Humanitarianism* (Ithaca, NY: Cornell University Press, 2011).

14. Craig Murphy, *International Organization and Industrial Change: Global Governance since 1850* (Cambridge, UK: Polity Press, 1994).

15. Robert O. Keohane and Joseph S. Nye, *Power and Interdependence: World Politics in Transition* (Boston: Little, Brown, 1977), 7.

16. Kishore Mahbubani, *The Great Convergence: Asia, the West, and the Logic of One World* (New York: Public Affairs, 2013), 3.

17. Commitments by 17 US states and 684 cities (representing over half of the US population) could stabilize US emissions at 2010 levels by 2020. See N. Lutsey and D. Sperling, "America's Bottom-Up Climate Change Mitigation Policy," *Energy Policy* 36, no. 2 (2008): 673–85; and B. Au et al., *Beyond a Global Deal: A UN+ Approach to Climate Governance* (Berlin: Global Governance 2020, 2011).

18. Richard N. Haass, *Foreign Policy Begins at Home: The Case for Putting America's House in Order* (New York: Basic Books, 2013), 5.

19. David Held and Anthony McGrew, with David Goldblatt and Jonathan Perraton, *Global Transformations: Politics, Economics, and Culture* (Palo Alto, CA: Stanford University Press, 1999).

20. Amit Bhaduri and Deepak Nayyar, *The Intelligent Person's Guide to Liberalization* (New Delhi: Penguin, 1996), 67.

21. C. A. Bayly, *The Birth of the Modern World 1780–1914* (Oxford: Blackwell, 2004).

22. Paul Hirst and Grahame Thompson, *Globalization in Question: The International Economy and the Possibilities of Governance* (Cambridge, UK: Polity Press, 1996).

23. Deborah D. Avant, Martha Finnemore, and Susan K. Sell, "Who Governs the Globe?" in *Who Governs the Globe?* ed. Deborah D. Avant, Martha Finnemore, and Susan K. Sell (Cambridge: Cambridge University Press, 2010), 4.

24. World Commission on the Social Dimension of Globalization, *A Fair Globalization: Creating Opportunities for All* (Geneva: International Labour Organization, 2004), xi.

25. Frances Stewart, "Global Aspects and Implications of Horizontal Inequalities: Inequalities Experienced by Muslims Worldwide," in *Global Governance, Poverty and Inequality*, ed. Jennifer Clapp and Rorden Wilkinson (London: Routledge, 2010), 265–94.

26. Samuel P. Huntington, *The Third Wave: Democratization in the Late Twentieth Century* (Norman: University of Oklahoma Press, 1991).

27. Sinclair, *Global Governance*, 57.

28. Kofi Annan, *Interventions: A Life in War and Peace* (New York: Penguin, 2012), 12.

29. Edward A. Fogarty, *States, Nonstate Actors, and Global Governance* (London: Routledge, 2013), 1 (emphasis in original).

30. Ian Bache and Matthew Flinders, eds., *Multi-Level Governance* (Oxford: Oxford University Press, 2004).

31. Data are from Union of International Associations, *Yearbook of International Organizations*, ed. 48, vol. 5 (Brussels: Union of International Associations, 2011), using the year closest to the end of the decade and including all INGO and IGO categories. Data for IGOs from 1920 to 1940 are from Michael Wallace and J. David Singer,

"Intergovernmental Organization in the Global System, 1815–1964: A Quantitative Description," *International Organization* 24, no. 2 (1970): 239–87. Comparable data for INGOs from 1920 to 1950 are unavailable.

32. Steve Charnovitz, "Two Centuries of Participation: NGOs and International Governance," *Michigan Journal of International Law* 18, no. 2 (1997): 190.

33. Kjell Skjelsbaek, "The Growth of International Nongovernmental Organization in the Twentieth Century," *International Organization* 25, no. 3 (1971): 429.

34. Sarianna M. Lundan, "The Coevolution of Transnational Corporations," *Indiana Journal of Global Legal Studies* 18, no. 2 (2011): 639–63.

35. See UN Conference on Trade and Development, *World Investment Report,* available at http://unctad.org/en/Pages/DIAE/World%20Investment%20Report/WIR -Series.aspx.

36. P. W. Anderson, "More Is Different: Broken Symmetry and the Nature of the Hierarchical Structure of Science," *Science* 177, no. 4047 (1972): 393–96.

37. James N. Rosenau, "Toward an Ontology for Global Governance," in *Approaches to Global Governance Theory,* ed. Martin Hewson and Timothy J. Sinclair (Albany: State University of New York Press, 1999), 293.

38. Ernst B. Haas, *Beyond the Nation-State: Functionalism and International Organization* (Palo Alto, CA: Stanford University Press, 1964).

39. Thomas G. Weiss, "What Happened to the Idea of World Government?" *International Studies Quarterly* 53, no. 2 (2009): 253–71.

40. Joseph Preston Barrata, *The Politics of World Federation,* vol. 2 (Westport, CT: Praeger, 2004), 534–35.

41. Anne-Marie Slaughter, *A New World Order* (Princeton, NJ: Princeton University Press, 2004), 8.

42. Michael Mandelbaum, *The Case for Goliath: How America Acts as the World's Government in the Twenty-First Century* (New York: Public Affairs, 2006); and Niall Ferguson, *Colossus: The Price of America's Empire* (New York: Penguin, 2004).

43. Alexander Wendt, "Why a World State Is Inevitable," *European Journal of International Relations* 9, no. 4 (2003): 491–542.

44. Daniel H. Deudney, *Bounding Power: Republican Security Theory from the Polis to the Global Village* (Princeton, NJ: Princeton University Press, 2007).

45. Richard Falk, "International Law and the Future," *Third World Quarterly* 27, no. 5 (2006): 727–37.

46. Dani Rodrik, "How Far Will International Economic Integration Go?" *Journal of Economic Perspectives* 14, no. 1 (2000): 177–86.

47. Campbell Craig, "The Resurgent Idea of World Government," *Ethics and International Affairs* 22, no. 2 (2008): 133–42.

48. Thomas G. Weiss, Kelsey Coolidge, and Conor Seyle, *Global Governance Is Not Sunset Industry* (Broomfield, CO: One Earth Future Foundation, 2013).

49. Robert Frost, "The Road Not Taken," available at www.poetryfoundation.org /poem/173536.

Chapter Two

1. Roger Normand and Sarah Zaidi, *Human Rights at the UN: The Political History of Universal Justice* (Bloomington: Indiana University Press, 2008); Julie Mertus, *The United Nations and Human Rights*, 2nd ed. (London: Routledge, 2009); and Bertrand G. Ramcharan, *Contemporary Human Rights Ideas* (London: Routledge, 2008).

2. Quoted by William Korey, *NGOs and the Universal Declaration of Human Rights: "A Curious Grapevine"* (New York: St. Martin's Press, 1998), 9.

3. Michael Ignatieff, *Human Rights as Politics and Idolatry*, ed. and intro. Amy Gutmann (Princeton, NJ: Princeton University Press, 2001), 5.

4. Bertrand G. Ramcharan, *The Human Rights Council* (London: Routledge, 2011).

5. Philip N. Howard and Muzammil M. Hussain, "The Role of Digital Media," *Journal of Democracy* 22, no. 3 (2011): 35–48.

6. Stephen Hopgood, *The Endtimes of Human Rights* (Ithaca, NY: Cornell University Press, 2013).

7. International Commission on Intervention and State Sovereignty, *The Responsibility to Protect* (Ottawa: International Development Research Centre, 2001).

8. For interpretations by commissioners, see Gareth Evans, *The Responsibility to Protect: Ending Mass Atrocity Crimes Once and for All* (Washington, DC: Brookings Institution, 2008); and Ramesh Thakur, *The United Nations, Peace and Security: From Collective Security to the Responsibility to Protect* (Cambridge: Cambridge University Press, 2006). See also Alex J. Bellamy, *Responsibility to Protect: The Global Effort to End Mass Atrocities* (Cambridge, UK: Polity Press, 2009); Anne Orford, *International Authority and the Responsibility to Protect* (Cambridge: Cambridge University Press, 2011); Aidan Hehir, *The Responsibility to Protect: Rhetoric, Reality and the Future of Humanitarian Intervention* (Basingstoke, UK: Palgrave Macmillan, 2012); and Thomas G. Weiss, *Humanitarian Intervention: Ideas in Action*, 2nd ed. (Cambridge, UK: Polity Press, 2012).

9. Gareth Evans, "Commission Diplomacy," in *The Oxford Handbook of Modern Diplomacy*, ed. Andrew F. Cooper, Jorge Heine, and Ramesh Thakur (Oxford: Oxford University Press, 2013), 289.

10. High-Level Panel on Threats, Challenges and Change, *A More Secure World: Our Shared Responsibility* (New York: United Nations, 2004), para. 203.

11. Kofi A. Annan, *In Larger Freedom: Towards Development, Security and Human Rights for All* (New York: United Nations, 2005).

12. *2005 World Summit Outcome*, UN document A/60/1, October 24, 2005, paras. 138–40.

13. Ban Ki-moon, *Implementing the Responsibility to Protect, Report of the Secretary-General*, UN document A/63/677, January 12, 2009.

14. Anne-Marie Slaughter, "A Day to Celebrate, but Hard Work Ahead," *Foreign Policy*, March 18, 2011, available at http://www.foreignpolicy.com/articles/2011/03/18/does_the_world_belong_in_libyas_war?page=0,7.

15. Greenberg Research, *The People on War Report* (Geneva: ICRC, 1999), xvi.

16. Francis M. Deng et al., *Sovereignty as Responsibility* (Washington, DC: Brookings Institution, 1995); and Thomas G. Weiss and David A. Korn, *Internal Displacement: Conceptualization and Its Consequences* (London: Routledge, 2006).

17. Cristina Badescu and Thomas G. Weiss, "Misrepresenting R2P and Advancing Norms: An Alternative Spiral?" *International Studies Perspectives* 11, no. 4 (2010): 354–74.

18. Madeleine K. Albright and S. Richard Williamson, *The United States and R2P: From Words to Action* (Washington, DC: US Institute of Peace, 2013), 16 and 10.

19. Taylor B. Seybolt, Jay D. Aronson, and Baruch Fischhoff, eds., *Counting Civilian Casualties: An Introduction to Recording and Estimating Nonmilitary Deaths in Conflict* (Oxford: Oxford University Press, 2013).

20. "Letter Dated 9 November 2011 from the Permanent Representative of Brazil to the United Nations Addressed to the Secretary-General," UN document A/66/551 -S/2011/701, 1.

21. Wolfgang Seibel, "R2P and German Foreign Policy 'after Libya,'" in *Norms and Practice of the Responsibility to Protect*, ed. C. Daase, J. Junk, and W. Seibel (London: Routledge, forthcoming).

22. S. Neil MacFarlane, *Intervention in Contemporary World Politics*, Adelphi Paper 350 (Oxford: Oxford University Press, 2002), 79.

23. Christine Bourloyannis, "The Security Council of the United Nations and the Implementation of International Humanitarian Law," *Denver Journal of International Law and Policy* 20, no. 3 (1993): 43.

24. Th. A. van Baarda, "The Involvement of the Security Council in Maintaining International Law," *Netherlands Quarterly of Human Rights* 12, no. 1 (1994): 140.

25. Stephen D. Krasner, *Sovereignty: Organized Hypocrisy* (Princeton, NJ: Princeton University Press, 1999).

26. David Cortright and George A. Lopez, eds., *The Sanctions Decade: Assessing UN Strategies in the 1990s* (Boulder, CO: Lynne Rienner, 2000).

27. Richard J. Goldstone and Adam Smith, *International Judicial Institutions* (London: Routledge, 2009).

28. Quoted in "Smoother Operator," *The Economist*, August 3, 2013, available at http://www.economist.com/node/319050.

29. Henry Kissinger, "The World Must Forge a New Order or Retreat into Chaos," *The Independent*, January 20, 2009, available at http://www.independent.co.uk/voices

/commentators/henry-kissinger-the-world-must-forge-a-new-order-or-retreat-to-chaos-1451416.html.

30. See Andrew F. Cooper and Ramesh Thakur, *Group of Twenty (G20)* (London: Routledge, 2013).

31. Jan N. Pieterse, "Global Rebalancing: Crisis and the East-South Turn," *Development and Change* 42, no. 1 (2011): 22–48.

32. Richard Jolly et al., *Be Outraged: There Are Alternatives* (Sussex, UK: Author, 2012), 53.

33. Craig N. Murphy, *International Organization and Industrial Change: Global Governance since 1850* (Cambridge, UK: Polity Press, 1994).

34. Robert I. Rotberg and Thomas G. Weiss, eds., *From Massacres to Genocide: The Media, Public Policy, and Humanitarian Crises* (Cambridge, MA: World Peace Foundation, 1996); and Nik Gowing, *Media Coverage: Help or Hindrance in Conflict Prevention?* (New York: Carnegie Commission on Preventing Deadly Conflict, 1997).

35. Rachel Carson, *Silent Spring* (Boston: Houghton Mifflin, 1962); and Donella H. Meadows, Dennis L. Meadows, J. Randers, and W. W. Behrens III, *The Limits To Growth* (New York: University Books, 1972).

36. Bjørn Lomborg, *The Skeptical Environmentalist* (Cambridge: Cambridge University Press, 2001); and Nigel Lawson, *An Appeal to Reason: A Cool Look at Global Warming* (London: Duckworth Overlook, 2008).

37. William D. Ruckelhaus, Lee M. Thomas, William K. Reilly, and Christine Todd Whitman, "A Republican Case for Climate Action," *New York Times*, August 2, 2013, available at http://www.nytimes.com/2013/08/02/opinion/a-republican-case-for-climate-action.html?_r=0.

38. Donella H. Meadows, Dennis L. Meadows, and J. Randers, *Limits to Growth: The 30-Year Update* (White River Junction, VT: Chelsea Green Publishing Company, 2004); and Graham Turner, *A Comparison of the Limits to Growth with Thirty Years of Reality*, CSIRO Working Paper Series 2008–09 (Canberra, Australia: Commonwealth Scientific and Industrial Research Organisation, 2008).

39. R. V. Cruz et al., "Asia," in IPCC, *Climate Change 2007: Impacts, Adaptation and Vulnerability—Contribution of Working Group II to the Fourth Assessment Report of the Intergovernmental Panel on Climate Change*, ed. M. L. Parry and O. F. Canziani (Cambridge: Cambridge University Press, 2007), 469–506.

40. G. Magrin et al., "Latin America," in IPCC, *Climate Change 2007: Impacts, Adaptation and Vulnerability—Contribution of Working Group II to the Fourth Assessment Report of the Intergovernmental Panel on Climate Change*, ed. M. L. Parry and O. F. Canziani (Cambridge: Cambridge University Press, 2007), 581–615.

41. Bert Bolin, *A History of the Science and Politics of Climate Change: The Role of the Intergovernmental Panel on Climate Change* (Cambridge: Cambridge University Press, 2008).

42. Nicholas Stern, *Stern Review on the Economics of Climate Change* (London: HM Treasury, 2007).

43. *National Security and the Threat of Climate Change* (Washington, DC: The CNA Corporation, 2007), 6. See also John D. Steinbruner, Paul C. Stern, and Jo L. Husbands, eds., *Climate and Social Stress: Implications for Security Analysis* (Washington, DC: National Research Council, 2013).

44. The United Nations Secretary-General's High-Level Panel on Global Sustainability, *Resilient People, Resilient Planet: A Future Worth Choosing* (New York: United Nations, 2012), 65–6.

45. Nadil Ajam, "The Case against a New International Environmental Organization," *Global Governance* 9, no. 3 (2003): 367–84.

46. Rorden Wilkinson, *What's Wrong with the WTO and How to Fix It* (Cambridge, UK: Polity Press, forthcoming); and James R. Vreeland, *The International Monetary Fund: Politics of Conditional Lending* (London: Routledge, 2007).

47. Text draws on Thomas G. Weiss and Martin Burke, "Legitimacy, Identity, and Climate Change: Moving from International to World Society," *Third World Quarterly* 32, no. 6 (2011): 1055–70.

48. Paul Hirst and Grahame Thompson, *Globalization in Question: The International Economy and the Possibilities of Governance* (Cambridge, UK: Polity Press, 1996); and David Held and Anthony McGrew, with David Goldblatt and Jonathan Perraton, *Global Transformations: Politics, Economics, and Culture* (Palo Alto, CA: Stanford University Press, 1999).

49. See essays by Thomas G. Weiss and Rorden Wilkinson, "Rethinking Global Governance: Complexity, Authority, Power, Change," *International Studies Quarterly* 58, no. 2 (2014): forthcoming; and "Global Governance to the Rescue: Saving International Relations?" *Global Governance* 20, no. 1 (2014): forthcoming.

50. Craig N. Murphy, "Global Governance: Poorly Done and Poorly Understood," *International Affairs* 76, no. 4 (2000): 789.

51. Yoshikazu Sakamoto, ed., *Global Transformations: Challenges to the State System* (Tokyo: United Nations University Press, 1992); Keith Krause and W. Andy Knight, eds., *State, Society and the UN System: Changing Perspectives on Multilateralism* (Tokyo: United Nations University Press, 1995); Robert W. Cox, ed., *The New Realism: Perspectives on Multilateralism and World Order* (Basingstoke, UK: Macmillan, 1997); Stephen Gill, ed., *Globalization, Democratization and Multilateralism* (London: Macmillan, 1997); Michael G. Schechter, ed., *Future Multilateralism: The Political and Social Framework* (London: Macmillan, 1999) and *Innovation in Multilateralism* (London: Macmillan, 1999).

52. Robert W. Cox, "Introduction," in *The New Realism: Perspectives on Multilateralism and World Order,* ed. Robert W. Cox (Basingstoke, UK: Macmillan, 1997), xvi.

53. John Gerard Ruggie, ed., *Multilateralism Matters: The Theory and Praxis of an Institutional Form* (New York: Columbia University Press, 1993).

54. Edward Newman, Ramesh Thakur, and John Tirman, eds., *Multilateralism under Challenge? Power, International Order, and Structural Change* (Tokyo: United Nations University Press, 2006).

55. Nayan Chanda, "Runaway Globalization without Governance," *Global Governance* 14, no. 2 (2008): 119–25.

56. Richard Peet, *Unholy Trinity: The IMF, World Bank and WTO* (London: Zed Books, 2003); and Louise Amoore, ed., *The Global Resistance Reader* (London: Routledge, 2005).

57. Diane Coyle, *Governing the Global Economy* (Cambridge, UK: Polity Press, 2000); and David Held and Antony McGrew, eds., *Governing Globalization* (Cambridge, UK: Polity Press, 2002).

58. Steven Pinker, *The Better Angels of Our Nature: Why Violence Has Declined* (New York: Viking, 2011), 129–88, 378–481. See also Joshua S. Goldstein, *Winning the War on War: The Decline of Armed Conflict Worldwide* (New York: Dutton, 2011).

Chapter Three

1. Figures are from UN Development Programme, *Sustainability and Equity: A Better Future for All, Human Development Report 2011* (New York: Palgrave Macmillan, 2011).

2. UN Development Programme, *The Rise of the South: Human Progress in a Diverse World, Human Development Report 2013* (New York: UNDP, 2013), 2.

3. Simon Hix, *What's Wrong with the European Union and How to Fix It* (Cambridge, UK: Polity Press, 2008), 23–4.

4. James B. Davies et al., "World Distribution of Household Wealth," *Discussion Paper No. 2008/03*, World Institute for Development Economics Research, UN University, February 2008.

5. Isabel Ortiz and Matthew Cummins, *Global Inequality: Beyond the Bottom Billion—A Rapid Review of Income Distribution in 141 Countries* (New York: UNICEF, 2011); and Erik S. Reinert, *How Rich Countries Got Rich and Why Poor Countries Stay Poor* (London: Public Affairs, 2007).

6. Branko Milanovic, *Worlds Apart: Measuring International and Global Inequality* (Princeton, NJ: Princeton University Press, 2005).

7. Reinert, *How Rich Countries Got Rich*.

8. Joseph E. Stiglitz, *The Price of Inequality: How Today's Divided Society Endangers Our Future* (New York: Norton, 2012).

9. UN Development Programme, *Human Development Report 2013*, 14.

10. David Hulme, *Global Poverty: How Global Governance Is Failing the Poor* (London: Routledge, 2010), 1.

11. Michael G. Schechter, *United Nations Global Conferences* (London: Routledge, 2005).

12. Elizabeth DeSombre, *Global Environmental Institutions* (London: Routledge, 2005).

13. Quoted by Pilita Clark, "Green Shift Grows, Deal or No Deal," *Financial Times*, November 19, 2011, available at http://www.ft.com/cms/s/0/ffbd7926-1087-11e1-8298 -00144feabdc0.html.

14. David Held, Angus Hervey, and Marika Theros, "Introduction," in *The Governance of Climate Change: Science, Economics, Politics and Ethics*, ed. David Held, Angus Hervey, and Marika Theros (Cambridge, UK: Polity Press, 2011), 9.

15. Sverker C. Jagers and Johannes Stripple, "Climate Governance beyond the State," *Global Governance* 9, no. 3 (2003): 385.

16. "Kyoto Opponents Hold Climate Talks," January 11, 2006. Available at http:// English.aljazeera.net/NR/exeres/5ED935AD-B7AF-4D66-A304-71BEBA760C15 .htm.

17. "Regional Greenhouse Gas Initiative (RGGI)," www.rggi.org.

18. International Energy Agency, *World Energy Outlook 2007* (Paris: IEA, 2007).

19. See "Rising Powers and the Future of Global Governance," guest editors Kevin Gray and Craig N. Murphy, *Third World Quarterly* 34, no. 2 (2013); and "Foreign Policy Strategies of Emerging Powers in a Multipolar World," guest editors Andrew F. Cooper and Daniel Flemes, *Third World Quarterly* 34, no. 6 (2013).

20. Climate Policy Initiative, *The Landscape of Climate Finance*, October 2011, available at http://climatepolicyinitiatiive.org/wp-contents/uploads/2011/10/The -Landscape-of-Climate-Finance-120120.pdf.

21. Tapio Kanninen, *Crisis of Global Sustainability* (London: Routledge, 2013).

22. Sven Van Kerckhoven, the University of Leuven, compiled these data from International Energy Agency publications; available at www.iea.org/publications /freepublications/publication/name,4010,en.html.

23. David Held, Charles Roger, and Eva-Maria Nag, "Introduction," in *Climate Governance in the Developing World*, ed. David Held, Charles Roger, and Eva-Maria Nag (Cambridge, UK: Polity Press 2013), 4.

24. Daniel M. Bodansky, *The Art and Craft of International Environmental Law* (Cambridge, MA: Harvard University Press, 2009), 1.

25. Simon Romero and John M. Broder, "Progress on the Sidelines as Rio Conference Ends," *New York Times*, June 24, 2012, available at http://www.nytimes.com /2012/06/24/world/americas/rio20-conference-ends-with-some-progress-on-the -sidelines.html.

26. World Commission on Environment and Development, *Our Common Future* (Oxford: Oxford University Press, 1987), 27.

27. John Vogler, "The Challenge of the Environment, Energy, and Climate Change," in *International Relations and the European Union*, ed. Christopher Hill and Michael Smith (New York: Oxford University Press, 2011), 349–79.

28. Ernst B. Haas, *The Uniting of Europe: Political, Social, and Economic Forces 1950–57* (Stanford, CA: Stanford University Press, 1958), 16.

29. Hendrik Spruyt, *The Sovereign State and Its Competitors* (Princeton, NJ: Princeton University Press, 1996).

30. Benedict Anderson, *Imagined Communities: Reflections on the Origin and Spread of Nationalism* (London: Verso, 1983).

31. Emanuel Adler, "Imagined (Security) Communities: Cognitive Regions in IR," *International Studies Quarterly* 39, no. 2 (1997): 255.

32. Alexander Wendt, "Collective Identity Formation and the International State," *American Political Science Review* 88, no. 2 (1994): 384–96.

33. David Held, Angus Hervey, and Marika Theros, eds., *The Governance of Climate Change: Science, Economics, Politics and Ethics* (Cambridge, UK: Polity Press, 2011).

34. Quoted by Koko Warner et al., "In Search of Shelter: Mapping the Effects of Climate Change on Human Migration and Displacement," CARE report, 2009, 2, available at http://ciesin.columbia.edu/documents/clim-migr-report-june09_media.pdf.

35. Arthur A. Stein, "Coordination and Collaboration: Regimes in an Anarchic World," *International Organization* 36, no. 2 (1982): 299–324.

36. For further discussion of these dilemmas, see Stein, "Coordination and Collaboration."

37. Paul D'Anieri, "International Organizations, Environmental Cooperation, and Regime Theory," in *International Organizations and Environmental Policy*, ed. R. V. Bartlett, P. A. Kurian, and M. Malik (Westport, CT: Greenwood Press, 1995), 153–70.

Chapter Four

1. Oran R. Young, *International Cooperation: Building Regimes for Natural Resources and the Environment* (Ithaca, NY: Cornell University Press, 1989), 32.

2. Konrad von Moltke, *Whither MEAs? The Role of International Environmental Management in the Trade and Environment Agenda* (Winnipeg, Canada: International Institute for Sustainable Development, 2001), 11.

3. Robert Dahl, "The Concept of Power," *Behavioral Science* 2, no. 3 (1957): 201–15.

4. Anne Mette Kjaer, *Governance* (Cambridge, UK: Polity Press, 2004), 205.

5. Michael Barnett and Raymond Duvall, "Introduction," in *Power in Global Governance*, ed. Michael Barnett and Raymond Duvall (Cambridge: Cambridge University Press, 2005), 3.

6. Sarah Collinson and Samir Elhawary, *Humanitarian Space: A Review of Trends and Issues*, HPG Report 32 (London: Overseas Development Institute, 2012), 2.

7. Timothy Sinclair, "Credit Rating Agencies," in *International Organization and Global Governance*, ed. Thomas G. Weiss and Rorden Wilkinson (Abingdon, UK: Routledge, 2013), 349–59.

8. Axel Marx et al., eds., *Private Standards and Global Governance: Economic, Legal and Political Perspectives* (Cheltenham, UK: Edward Elgar, 2012).

9. Danielle A. Zach, Conor Seyle, and Jens Vestergaard Madsen, *Burden-Sharing Multilevel Governance: A Study of the Contact Group on Piracy off the Coast of Somalia* (Broomfield, CO: One Earth Future Foundation, 2013).

10. Thomas Risse, "Social Constructivism and European Integration," in *European Integration Theory*, 2nd ed., ed. Antje Wiener and Thomas Diez (Oxford: Oxford University Press, 2009), 145.

11. Deborah D. Avant, Martha Finnemore, and Susan K. Sell, "Who Governs the Globe?" in *Who Governs the Globe?* ed. Deborah D. Avant, Martha Finnemore, and Susan K. Sell (Cambridge: Cambridge University Press, 2010), 2.

12. David Singh Grewal, *Network Power: The Social Dynamics of Globalization* (New Haven, CT: Yale University Press, 2008), 9.

13. James N. Rosenau, "Governance in the Twenty-First Century," *Global Governance* 1, no. 1 (1995): 13–43.

14. Inge Kaul, Isabelle Grunberg, and Marc A. Stern, eds., *Global Public Goods: International Cooperation in the 21st Century* (Oxford: Oxford University Press, 1999); and Inge Kaul et al., eds., *Global Public Goods: Managing Globalization* (Oxford: Oxford University Press, 2003).

15. Scott Barrett, *Why Cooperate? The Incentive to Supply Global Public Goods* (Oxford: Oxford University Press, 2007), 2.

16. Barrett, *Why Cooperate?*, 8–9, emphasis in original.

17. Daniel Deudney and G. John Ikenberry, "The Myth of the Autocratic Revival: Why Liberal Democracy Will Prevail," *Foreign Affairs* 88, no. 1 (2009): 79.

18. John Mearsheimer, "The False Promise of International Institutions," *International Security* 19, no. 3 (1994/95): 5–49.

19. Hans J. Morgenthau, *Politics among Nations: The Struggle for Power and Peace*, 6th ed. (New York: McGraw-Hill, 1985), 536.

20. Kenneth N. Waltz, *Man, the State, and War* (New York: Columbia University Press, 1959), 238.

21. Michael Walzer, *Spheres of Justice: A Defense of Pluralism and Equality* (New York: Basic Books, 1983).

22. Wiener and Diez, *European Integration Theory*.

23. Jan Zielonka, *Can Europe Survive?* (Cambridge, UK: Polity Press, forthcoming).

24. Thomas Hale, David Held, and Kevin Young, *Gridlock: Why Global Cooperation Is Failing When We Need It Most* (Cambridge, UK: Polity Press, 2013).

25. Dan Plesch, *America, Hitler and the UN* (London: Tauris, 2011); and Thomas G. Weiss, "Renewing Washington's Multilateral Leadership," *Global Governance* 18, no. 3 (2012): 253–66.

26. E. H. Carr, *What Is History?* (London: Pelican, 1961), 62.

27. Andrew J. Williams, Amelia Hadfield, and J. Simon Rofe, *International History and International Relations* (London: Routledge, 2012), 3.

28. Hans Singer, "An Historical Perspective," in *The UN and the Bretton Woods Institutions: New Challenges for the Twenty-First Century*, ed. Mahbub ul Haq et al. (London: Macmillan, 1995), 19.

29. Kishore Mahbubani, *The Great Convergence: Asia, the West, and the Logic of One World* (New York: Public Affairs, 2013), 224.

30. Robert O'Brien, Anne-Marie Goetz, Jan Aart Scholte, and Marc Williams, *Contesting Global Governance: Multilateral Economic Institutions and Global Social Movements* (Cambridge: Cambridge University Press, 2000).

31. Adam Roberts and Benedict Kingsbury, "Introduction: The UN's Roles in International Society since 1945," in *United Nations: Divided World*, 2nd ed., ed. Adam Roberts and Benedict Kingsbury (Oxford: Oxford University Press, 1993), 1.

32. Edward Newman, Ramesh Thakur, and John Tirman, eds., *Multilateralism under Challenge? Power, International Order, and Structural Change* (Tokyo: United Nations University Press, 2006).

33. Hale, Held, and Young, *Gridlock*, 34.

34. Anne-Marie Slaughter, *A New World Order* (Princeton, NJ: Princeton University Press, 2004).

35. Craig Murphy and JoAnne Yates, *The International Standards Organization* (London: Routledge, 2009).

36. A. Prakash and M. Potoski, "Racing to the Bottom? Trade, Environmental Governance, and ISO 14001," *American Journal of Political Science* 50, no. 2 (2006): 350–64.

37. Maurice Bertrand, *The Third Generation World Organization* (Dordrecht, The Netherlands: Martinus Nijhoff, 1989), 27.

38. Besides Jean Pictet, *The Fundamental Principles of the Red Cross* (Geneva: ICRC, 1979), see David P. Forsythe, *The Humanitarians: The International Committee of the Red Cross* (Cambridge: Cambridge University Press, 2005); and Thomas G. Weiss, "Principles, Politics, and Humanitarian Action," *Ethics and International Affairs*, no. 13 (1999): 1–22.

39. John Mathiason, *Internet Governance: The New Frontier of Global Institutions* (London: Routledge, 2009).

40. Susan V. Scott and Markos Zachariadis, *The Society for Worldwide Interbank Financial Telecommunication (SWIFT): Cooperative Governance for Network Innovation, Standards, and Community* (London: Routledge, 2014).

41. John Gerard Ruggie, "What Makes the World Hang Together? Neo-Utilitarianism and the Social Constructivist Challenge," *International Organization* 52, no. 4 (1998): 855–85.

42. Kofi Annan, *Interventions: A Life in War and Peace* (New York: Penguin, 2012), 144.

Chapter Five

1. Hedley Bull, *The Anarchical Society: A Study of Order in World Politics*, 3rd ed. (New York: Columbia University Press, 2002), 13.

2. Barry Buzan, *From International to World Society: English School Theory and the Social Structure of Globalisation* (Cambridge: Cambridge University Press, 2004).

3. See, for example, Global Witness's criticism, which ultimately led to the withdrawal of Global Witness from the process, available at http://www.globalwitness.org /campaigns/conflict/conflict-diamonds/kimberley-process.

4. Daniel W. Drezner, "'Good Enough' Global Governance and International Finance," *Foreign Policy Blogs*, January 30, 2013, available at http://drezner .foreignpolicy.com/posts/2013/01/30/good_enough_global_governance_and _international_finance.

5. David Held and Charles Roger, eds., *Global Governance at Risk* (Cambridge, UK: Polity Press, 2013).

6. Thomas G. Weiss, *Global Governance: A "Philadelphia Moment"?* (Broomfield, CO: One Earth Future, 2013).

7. The annual publication from the Center for International Cooperation has details, the most recent being *Annual Review of Global Peace Operations 2013* (Boulder, CO: Lynne Rienner, 2013).

8. See, for example, Peter Romaniuk, *Multilateral Counter-Terrorism: The Global Politics of Cooperation and Contestation* (London: Routledge, 2010); and Frank Madsen, *Transnational Organized Crime* (London: Routledge, 2009).

9. Rorden Wilkinson, *What's Wrong with the WTO and How to Fix It* (Cambridge, UK: Polity Press, forthcoming).

10. Mark Doyle, "African Remittances Outweigh Western Aid," BBC News, available at http://www.bbc.co.uk/news/world-africa-22169474.

11. For example, see Sophie Harman, *Global Health Governance* (London: Routledge, 2012); and Franklyn Lisk, *Global Institutions and the HIV/AIDS Epidemic: Responding to an International Crisis* (London: Routledge, 2010).

12. Deborah D. Avant, Martha Finnemore, and Susan K. Sell, "Who Governs the Globe?" in *Who Governs the Globe?* ed. Deborah D. Avant, Martha Finnemore, and Susan K. Sell (Cambridge: Cambridge University Press, 2010), 5.

13. Peter Willetts, *Non-Governmental Organizations in World Politics: The Construction of Global Governance* (London: Routledge, 2011), wishes to abandon the terminology because supposedly it reinforces the centrality of states.

14. Catia Gregoratti, *The Global Compact* (London: Routledge, forthcoming); and Oliver Williams, *Corporate Social Responsibility* (London: Routledge, 2013).

15. John Gerard Ruggie, "global_governance.net: The Global Compact as Learning Network," *Global Governance* 7, no. 4 (2001): 371–78.

16. High-Level Panel of Eminent Persons on the Post-2015 Development Agenda, *A New Global Partnership: Eradicate Poverty and Transform Economies through Sustainable Development* (New York: United Nations, 2013), available at http://www.post2015hlp .org/wp-content/uploads/2013/05/UN-Report.pdf.

17. *Now for the Long Term: The Report of the Oxford Martin Commission for Future Generations,* October 2013, available at http://www.oxfordmartin.ox.ac.uk/downloads /commission/Oxford_Martin_Now_for_the_Long_Term.pdf.

18. Inis L. Claude, Jr., *Swords into Plowshares: The Problems and Prospects of International Organization* (New York: Random House, 1956); and "Peace and Security: Prospective Roles for the Two United Nations," *Global Governance* 2, no. 3 (1996): 289–98.

19. Thomas G. Weiss, Tatiana Carayannis, and Richard Jolly, "The 'Third' United Nations," *Global Governance* 15, no. 1 (2009): 123–42.

20. Kofi A. Annan, "Introduction," in *"We the Peoples": A UN for the 21st Century* (Boulder, CO: Paradigm Publishers, forthcoming).

21. Abraham Chayes and Antonia H. Chayes, *The New Sovereignty: Compliance with International Regulatory Agreements* (Cambridge, MA: Harvard University Press, 1995).

22. S. Girma, "Absorptive Capacity and Productivity Spillovers from FDI: A Threshold Regression Analysis," *Oxford Bulletin of Economics and Statistics* 67, no. 3 (2005): 281–306; X. Li and X. Liu, "Foreign Direct Investment and Economic Growth: An Increasingly Endogenous Relationship," *World Development* 33, no. 3 (2005): 393–407; H. Lin and R.-S. Yeh, "The Interdependence between FDI and R&D: An Application of an Endogenous Switching Model to Taiwan's Electronics Industry," *Applied Economics* 37, no. 15 (2005): 1789–99; and P. M. Romer, "Endogenous Technological Change," *Journal of Political Economy* 98, no. 5 (1990): 71–102.

23. Chuck C. Y. Kwok and Solomon Tadesse, "The MNC as an Agent of Change for Host-Country Institutions: FDI and Corruption," *Journal of International Business Studies* 37, no. 6 (2006): 767–85.

24. See Andrew F. Cooper and Ramesh Thakur, *Group of Twenty (G20)* (London: Routledge, 2013).

25. Thomas S. Kuhn, *The Structure of Scientific Revolutions*, 2nd ed. (Chicago: University of Chicago Press, 1970), 4, 53.

26. Kalevi J. Holsti, *Taming the Sovereigns: Institutional Change in International Politics* (Cambridge: Cambridge University Press, 2004), 8.

27. William Shakespeare, *Hamlet*, Act III, Scene II.

28. Hans J. Morgenthau, *The Restoration of American Politics* (Chicago: University of Chicago Press, 1962), and *Politics among Nations* (New York: Knopf, 1960); and Reinhold Niebuhr, *Structure of Nations and Empires: A Study of the Recurring Patterns and Problems of the Political Order in Relation to the Unique Problems of the Nuclear Age* (New York: Scribner's, 1959).

29. Edward Hallett Carr, *The Twenty Years' Crisis, 1919–1939* (New York: Harper Torchbooks, 1964), 108.

30. Oscar Wilde, "The Soul of Man under Socialism," in *Selected Essays and Poems* (London: Penguin, 1954 [1891]), 34.

31. Thomas G. Weiss, *What's Wrong with the United Nations and How to Fix It*, 2nd ed. (Cambridge, UK: Polity Press, 2013).

32. Andrew Hurrell, "Foreword to the Third Edition," in Hedley Bull, *The Anarchical Society* (New York: Columbia University Press, 2002), xiii.

33. Elise Boulding, interview in Needham, Massachusetts, by the author, April 16, 2001. *The Complete Oral History Transcripts from UN Voices, CD-ROM* (New York: United Nations Intellectual History Project, 2007).

34. Tony Judt, *Postwar: A History of Europe since 1945* (London: Vintage Books, 2010), 21.

35. Nicolas Berggruen and Nathan Gardels, "The Next Europe: Toward a Federal Union," *Foreign Affairs* 92, no. 4 (2013): 134–42.

36. Andrew Moravcsik, "Europe, the Second Superpower," *Current History* 109 (March 2010): 91–98.

37. Simon Hix, *What's Wrong with the European Union and How to Fix It* (Cambridge, UK: Polity Press, 2008), 25.

38. Jean Monnet, *Memoirs* (New York: Doubleday, 1978).

39. Altiero Spinelli, *The Eurocrats: Conflict and Crisis in the European Community* (Baltimore, MD: Johns Hopkins University Press, 1966).

40. Mark Corner, *The Binding of Nations: From European Union to World Union* (Basingstoke, UK: Palgrave Macmillan, 2010), 205 (emphasis in original).

41. Quoted by Cass R. Sunstein, "An Original Thinker of Our Time," *New York Review of Books*, May 23, 2013.

42. Thomas Hobbes, *Leviathan* (New York: Touchstone, 1997 [1651]), 100.

43. Richard Beardsworth, *Cosmopolitanism and International Relations Theory* (Cambridge, UK: Polity Press, 2011).

44. Daniele Archibugi and David Held, eds., *Cosmopolitan Democracy: An Agenda for a New World* (Cambridge, UK: Polity Press, 1995).

45. Jessica T. Mathews, "The Power Shift," *Foreign Affairs* 76, no. 1 (1997): 61.

46. Ian Goldin, *Divided Nations: Why Global Governance Is Failing and What We Can Do about It* (Oxford: Oxford University Press, 2013), 166–67.

47. Thomas Hale, David Held, and Kevin Young, *Gridlock: Why Global Cooperation Is Failing When We Need It Most* (Cambridge, UK: Polity Press, 2013), 48.

48. William D. Ruckelhaus, Lee M. Thomas, William K. Reilly, and Christine Todd Whitman, "A Republican Case for Climate Action," *New York Times*, August 2, 2013.

49. Quoted by Thomas Friedman, *Hot, Flat and Crowded: Why We Need a Green Revolution—and How It Can Renew America* (New York: Farrar, Straus and Giroux, 2008), 438.

50. Peter B. Evans, Dietrich Rueschemeyer, and Theda Skocpol, eds., *Bringing the State Back In* (Cambridge: Cambridge University Press, 1985).

51. British Broadcasting Company, "Higgs Boson–Like Particle Discovery Claimed at LHC," July 4, 2012, available at http://www.bbc.co.uk/news/world-middle-east-11414483.

52. H. G. Wells, *The Shape of Things to Come*, 1933, Gutenberg Project electronic book, 1.

✳
SUGGESTED READINGS

The fundamentals of global governance are introduced by Timothy J. Sinclair, *Global Governance* (Cambridge, UK: Polity Press, 2012), and Anne Mette Kjaer, *Governance* (Cambridge, UK: Polity Press, 2004); the author's in-depth treatment is Thomas G. Weiss, *Global Governance: Why? What? Whither?* (Cambridge, UK: Polity Press, 2013). Additional insights are found in Ian Goldin, *Divided Nations: Why Global Governance Is Failing and What We Can Do about It* (Oxford: Oxford University Press, 2013); Thomas Hale, David Held, and Kevin Young, *Gridlock: Why Global Cooperation Is Failing When We Need It Most* (Cambridge, UK: Polity Press, 2013); Edward A. Fogarty, *States, Nonstate Actors, and Global Governance* (London: Routledge, 2013); Deborah D. Avant, Martha Finnemore, and Susan K. Sell, eds., *Who Governs the Globe?* (Cambridge: Cambridge University Press, 2010); Thomas G. Weiss and Ramesh Thakur, *Global Governance and the UN: An Unfinished Journey* (Bloomington: Indiana University Press, 2010); David Singh Grewal, *Network Power: The Social Dynamics of Globalization* (New Haven, CT: Yale University Press, 2008); Scott Barrett, *Why Cooperate? The Incentive to Supply Global Public Goods* (Oxford: Oxford University Press, 2007); Michael Barnett and Raymond Duvall, eds., *Power in Global Governance* (Cambridge: Cambridge University Press, 2005); and Craig N. Murphy, *International Organization and Industrial Change: Global Governance since 1850* (Cambridge, UK: Polity Press, 1994). *Global Governance: A Review of Multilateralism and International Organizations* is a quarterly journal published since 1995.

State sovereignty and its routine violations are explained by Stephen D. Krasner, *Sovereignty: Organized Hypocrisy* (Princeton, NJ: Princeton University Press, 1999). Kalevi J. Holsti, in *Taming the Sovereigns: Institutional Change in International Politics* (Cambridge: Cambridge University Press, 2004), discusses continuity and change for this essential topic.

Two concrete cases figure prominently in these pages. For climate change, readers should consult Tapio Kanninen, *Crisis of Global Sustainability* (London: Routledge, 2013); David Held, Angus Hervey, and Marika Theros, eds., *The Governance of Climate Change: Science, Economics, Politics and Ethics* (Cambridge, UK: Polity Press, 2011); Peter Newell and Harriet A. Bulkeley, *Governing Climate Change* (London: Routledge, 2010); Nico Schrijver, *Development without Destruction: The UN and Global Resource Management* (Bloomington: Indiana University Press, 2010); and the voluminous reports from the Intergovernmental Panel on Climate Change, available at http://www.ipcc.ch/. For opposing views, see Nigel Lawson, *An Appeal to Reason: A Cool Look at Global Warming* (London: Duckworth Overlook, 2008); and Bjørn Lomborg, *The Skeptical Environmentalist* (Cambridge: Cambridge University Press, 2001). For the European Union, useful starting points are Simon Hix, *What's Wrong with the European Union and How to Fix It* (Cambridge, UK: Polity Press, 2008); Clive Archer, *The European Union* (London: Routledge, 2007); and Antje Wiener and Thomas Diez, eds., *European Integration Theory*, 2nd ed. (Oxford: Oxford University Press, 2009). A forward-looking interpretation is Mark Corner, *The Binding of Nations: From European Union to World Union* (Houndsmills, Basingstoke, UK: Palgrave Macmillan, 2010); and a somber interpretation is Jan Zielonka, *Is the EU Doomed?* (Cambridge, UK: Polity Press, forthcoming).

Global institutions are numerous, complex, and far-flung, but introductions to many are found in the fifty chapters of Thomas G. Weiss and Rorden Wilkinson, eds., *International Organization and Global Governance* (London: Routledge, 2014). More comprehensive overviews of the most prominent IGOs and NGOs mentioned throughout this book are found in the Routledge Global Institutions Series, edited by Weiss and Wilkinson.

The most essential global institutions that should work better are part of the universal-membership UN system. Two authoritative compendia on legal and political perspectives are Bruno Simma, ed., *The Charter of the United Nations: A Commentary*, 2nd ed. (Oxford: Oxford University Press, 2002), and Thomas G. Weiss and Sam Daws, eds., *The Oxford Handbook on the United Nations* (Oxford: Oxford University Press, 2007). Two textbooks are José E. Alvarez, *International Organizations as Law-Makers* (Oxford: Oxford University Press, 2005); and Thomas G. Weiss, David P. Forsythe, Roger A. Coate, and Kelly-Kate Pease, *The United Nations and Changing World Politics*, 7th ed. (Boulder, CO: Westview, 2014). A harsher perspective is Thomas G. Weiss, *What's Wrong with the United Nations and How to Fix It*, 2nd ed. (Cambridge, UK: Polity Press, 2012). For the synthesis of ten years of research about the intellectual history of the world organization, see Richard Jolly, Louis Emmerij, and Thomas G. Weiss, *UN Ideas That Changed the World* (Bloomington: Indiana University Press, 2009).

A discussion of world government could begin with the English School's discussions of "international society" in Hedley Bull, *The Anarchical Society: A Study of Order in World Politics* (New York: Columbia University Press, 1977); in updates by Barry Buzan, *From International to World Society: English School Theory and the Social Structure of Globalisation* (Cambridge: Cambridge University Press, 2004); and Robert Jackson, in *The Global Covenant: Human Conduct in a World of States* (Oxford: Oxford University Press, 2000). Daniel H. Deudney, *Bounding Power: Republican Security Theory from the Polis to the Global Village* (Princeton, NJ: Princeton University Press, 2007) seeks to bridge realism and hierarchy. A contemporary plea for limited world government is James Yunker, *The Idea of World Government: From Ancient Times to the Twenty-First Century* (London: Routledge, 2011). A historical treatment is Mark Mazower, *Governing the World: The History of an Idea* (New York: Penguin, 2012).

INDEX

ABOUT THE AUTHOR

Thomas G. Weiss is Presidential Professor of Political Science and Director Emeritus of the Ralph Bunche Institute for International Studies at The City University of New York's Graduate Center, and Research Professor at SOAS, University of London. While completing this book, he was a resident fellow at the University of Konstanz's Kulturwissenschaftliches Kolleg and at the University of Leuven's Centre for Global Governance Studies as well as a non-resident fellow at the One Earth Future Foundation. In the previous decade, he directed the United Nations Intellectual History Project (1999–2010) and was president of the International Studies Association (2009–2010), chair of the Academic Council on the United Nations System (2006–2009), editor of *Global Governance* (2000–2005), and research director of the International Commission on Intervention and State Sovereignty (2000–2002). He has written extensively about multilateral approaches to international peace and security, humanitarian action, and sustainable development. His recent single-authored books include *Global Governance: Why? What? Whither* (2013); *Humanitarian Business* (2013); *What's Wrong with the United Nations and How to Fix It* (2012); *Humanitarian Intervention: Ideas in Action* (2012); and *Thinking about Global Governance: Why People and Ideas Matter* (2011).